The Mormon Art of War

A Complementation of Sun Tzu's *The Art of War*, Containing his Entire Ancient Treatise

By Kelly Gneiting

Foreword by Roy Varga

Afterword by Farley Anderson

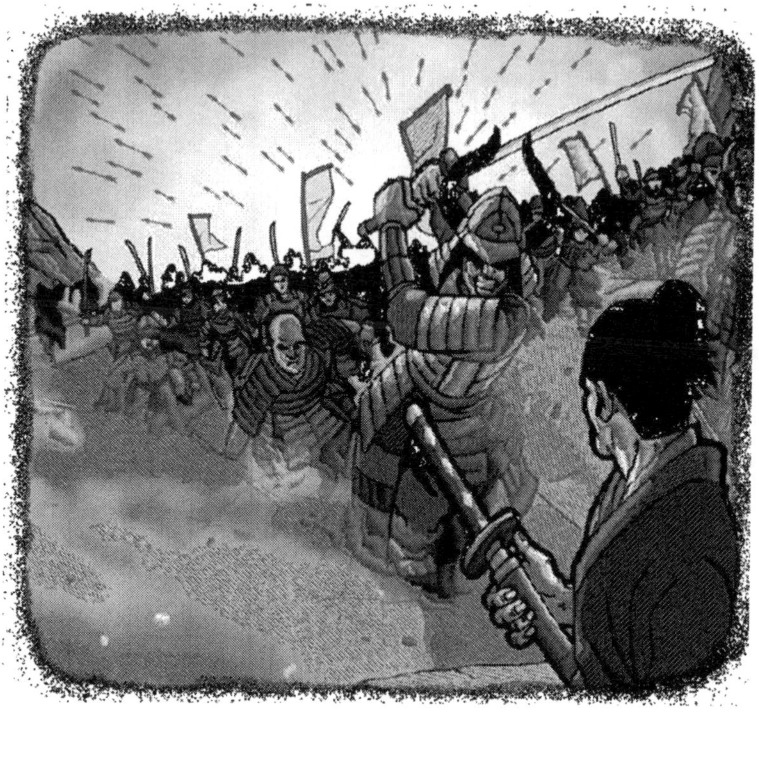

About the Front Cover Image

Sun Tzu, in the forefront, considered war as a necessary evil that must be avoided whenever possible. He notes that "war is like fire; people who do not lay down their arms will die by their arms."

Hence his teachings that, "...to win one hundred victories in one hundred battles is not the acme of skill. To subdue the enemy *without fighting* is the acme of skill."

Captain Moroni in the Book of Mormon understood these principles and always worked for a peaceful reconciliation. But when peace wasn't possible without succumbing to tyranny, he applied Sun Tzu's principles in war, as well as the 24 additional principles outlined in this book—principles which allow certain victory, for:

> "...behold he is mightier than all the earth, then why not mightier than Laban and his fifty, yea, or even than his tens of thousands?" (1 Nephi 4:1)

Copyright © 2012

Kelly Gneiting

Dedicated to those who will yet hoist the Title of Liberty

FOREWORD
By Roy Varga

Kelly Gneiting has written a well thought-out book that addresses a seldom thought of aspect of war, comparing the ancient writings of the Chinese military leader Sun Tzu to the more modern religious teachings of the Book of Mormon.

Gneiting's approach introduces the reader to his faith's view of war. As a Catholic, I found his book highly interesting since I had very little knowledge of the Mormon religion. He not only explains in detail aspects of Mormon viewpoints on war, but also refers to the Bible and our nation's Founders. This helps readers find familiarity with the various concepts and principles he brings forward. I found this approach very helpful and straightforward as it leads the reader instructively throughout the book.

I've read a lot of books and I can't remember anyone approaching war from Gneiting's viewpoint. I think Kelly hits the nail on the head, and The Book of Mormon's Art of War should get people thinking on where our country is going from this special and very important point of view.

> **I, [name], do solemnly swear (or affirm) that I will support and defend the Constitution of the United States against all enemies, foreign and domestic; that I will bear true faith and allegiance to the same; that I take this obligation freely, without any mental reservation or purpose of evasion; and that I will well and faithfully discharge the duties of the office on which I am about to enter. So help me God.**

As a veteran I took this oath at the beginning of my military career and each time I reenlisted. It is an oath to defend the Constitution—not support foreign entities such as the United Nations nor undeclared wars or "police actions." Because of this, I was very interested in Gneiting's comparison between Sun Tzu's Art of War and the Book of Mormon's Art of War. Readers can easily see similarities between not only these two philosophies as presented by the author, but can also relate to how the nation's Founders believed our foreign policy, military force and alliances should be approached and viewed. The author clearly shows the Founder's viewpoints on religion, foreign policy, and alliances through quotes by George Washington, Charles Pinckney, Thomas Jefferson and other Founders. He also quotes more modern leaders such as Ezra Taft Benson and Robert A. Taft.

One conclusion can be certain from reading Gneiting's book: Our nation's Founders followed a policy more in keeping with the principles of The Book of Mormon Art of War concerning foreign policy, military usage and alliances than American leaders of today.

This book is a useful tool not only as historical research or religious learning, but also as hope for present and future political leaders at all levels of government.

Gneiting's book is definitely a must read for anyone concerned with America's future.

Roy Varga, Cheyenne, Wyoming
Wyoming State Coordinator
Independent American Party

The Book of Mormon's *Art of War*

A Complementation of Sun Tzu's The Art of War, Containing his Entire Ancient Treatise

Table of Contents

Dedication & Introduction 13

    The Purpose of the Book of Mormon's Recordings of Wars 16

    Who was Mormon? 21

    Are War Stories Actual Scripture? 27

    War is Victory to Satan 30

    Sun Tzu's Art of War 44

    A Word About the Enemy 46

    The Philosophies of Tao Te Ching 53

    The Acme of Skill: Understanding, Diffusing, Conquering 55

The Vital Role of the Latter-day Lamanites 63

Jesus Christ' Foreordination of the Indian People, as recorded in 3 Nephi 21 92

Sun Tzu's The Art of War 105

    I. Laying Plans 105

    II. Waging War 110

    III. Attack by Strategem 114

    IV. Tactical Dispositions 119

    V. Energy 122

    VI. Weak Points and Strong 126

    VII. Maneuvering 132

    VIII. Variations in Tactics 139

    IX. The Army on the March 141

    X. Terrain 149

    XI. The Nine Situations 155

    XII. The Attack by Fire 167

    XIII. The Use of Spies 171

The Book of Mormon's Art of War 176

   What is 'the Strength of the Lord'? 176

      Principle 1 179

         Fighting "in the strength of the Lord" will always end in victory; without the Strength of the Lord, the Wicked destroy the Wicked, and Victory is decided by the Strength and Cunning of Man 179

      Principle 2 150

         Those who Gain The Strength of the Lord must make a Covenant or Oath to "maintain their rights (liberty), and their religion (as Christians)." (Alma 46:20) 150

   Entering War: Determining Your Enemy 187

      Principle 3 187

         War is only Justified in the Defense of Life, Property, and Liberty, including the People's Rights of Religion, and this After all other Reasonable Efforts for Peace have been Pursued 187

      Principle 4 191

         "Inasmuch as ye are not guilty of the first offense, neither the second, ye shall not suffer yourselves to be slain by the hands of your enemies" (Alma 43:46) 191

      Principle 5 194

"The inward vessel shall be cleansed first... even the great head of our government." (Alma 60:23-24) 194

Principle 6 198

"...whosoever [will] not take up arms in the defence of their country, but [will] fight against it, [are to be] put to death" (Alma 62:9)..198

Engaged in War: Interacting with the Enemy 202

Principle 7 202

Love for Your Fellowman is One's Motivation for Going into Battle. Pray for Your Deliverance, but also for your Enemies, Do not Delight in Killing 202

Principle 8 207

Your Leaders Must be Mighty Men of Humility, Faith, and Prayer (who make it Perfectly Clear within the Ranks as to the Cause for Which they are Fighting)..........207

Principle 9 211

Use Strategy, which involves Deceit ("Attack him where he is unprepared, appear where you are not expected" from Sun Tzu)..211

Principle 10 212

The Most Effective Means of Defense is to Fortify Areas of Possible Invasion...212

Principle 11 217

Confronting a Potential Enemy's Intent may be Necessary, with Good Judgment, to Ascertain their Plans 217

Principle 12 220

Make Use of Spies 220

Principle 13 221

Utilize Those Men of God With The Spirit of Prophecy, and are able to "inquire of the Lord" as to Specific war Strategies 221

Principle 14 224

Prepare Adequate Weapons for War................................224

Principle 15 225

During Actual Battle, Put your Trust in the Strength of the Lord, and have Courage, because of your Cause 225

Principle 16 228

God is the Order-Giver: He Controls the Laws of Mercy and Justice According to his Omniscient Foreknowledge. Be Obedient to God!..............................228

Principle 17 235

Don't Fear Death, Value your Liberty More than your Life...235

Principle 18 239

To Kill the Leader of an Enemy's Army Privily is to Gain Great Advantage 239

Principle 19 242

During Pivotal Moments, the Leader Must Inspire His Soldiers with Memorable and Inspirational Remarks 242

Principle 20 248

Respect the Rights and Freedoms on Others to NOT engage in Bloodshed, Who have made a Covenant of Peace 248

Principle 21 254

Let Your Enemy do your Work, when Possible 254

Ending War: Transitioning into Peace 255

Principle 22 255

Preach the Word of God to Prisoners of War 255

Principle 23 258

Captors are to be Released After they have Made a Covenant of Peace, Otherwise they are to be Put to Death 258

Principle 24 261

After a War is a Time of Humility, Fasting and Prayer, Giving Thanksgiving to God for the Victory, and to Mourn Lost Kindred 261

The Kingdom of God, by Brigham Young 264

United States Foreign Policy, By Ezra Taft Benson....................289

Constitutional State Militia BILL (Idaho example for all states) 322

AFTERWORD 328

Dedication & Introduction

Onward, Christian soldiers! Marching as to war,
With the cross of Jesus Going on before.
Christ, the royal Master, Leads against the foe;
Forward into battle, See his banners go!

At the sign of triumph Satan's host doth flee;
On, then, Christian soldiers, On to victory.
Hell's foundations quiver At the shout of praise;
Brothers, lift your voices, Loud your anthems raise.

Onward, Christian soldiers! Marching as to war,
With the cross of Jesus Going on before.
(19 Century English Hymn)

This book is dedicated to those who, as some future time, will lead others in *the strength of the Lord*, just as Alma, Moroni, Gidgiddoni, Helaman, and many others did in the Book of Mormon—a book for our day. It is evident that a large portion of these future leaders will be among the Latter-day Lamanites who will go forth "as a lion among the beasts of the forest, and as a young lion among the flocks of sheep, who, if he goeth through both treadeth down and teareth in pieces," (3rd Nephi 20:16) a people whom "I [the Lord] will make thy horn iron, and I will make thy hoofs brass. And thou shalt beat in pieces many people…" (3rd Nephi 20:19)

In his Fifth Annual Address to Congress, given in Philadelphia on December 3, 1793, George Washington stated:

> "There is a rank due to the United States among nations, which will be withheld, if not absolutely lost, by the reputation of weakness. If we desire to avoid insult, we must be able to repel it; if we desire to secure the peace—one of the most powerful instruments of our rising prosperity, it must be known that we are at all times ready for war."

Washington's advice on how best to keep peace is thus in two parts: (1) we must be ready for war, and (2) just as important, the enemy must know we are ready.

This is the crowing principle in defending Zion, and securing a free society from the intrusion of outside forces. The Latter-day Lamanites, or American Indians, are the descendants of the Book of Mormon people. In addition, the Book of Mormon itself was "written to the Lamanites," as indicated in the Book of

Mormon's Title Page. Hence it seems reasonable that any professional work or study of the Book of Mormon must be dedicated to this "remnant of Joseph," or, along with the Jews, "remnant of Jacob," both spoken of in the book itself many times (see Alma 46:23-24, Ether 13:6, 3 Nephi 21:23).

After all, many Latter-day Lamanites are the descendents of Helaman's stripling warriors who *in the strength of the Lord* defeated mighty armies in two different battles without the loss of even one life. It is said that these Indian ancestors:

> "...entered into a covenant to fight for the liberty of the Nephites, yea, to protect the land unto the laying down of their lives; yea, even they covenanted that they never would give up their liberty, but they would fight in all cases to protect the Nephites and themselves from bondage... (Alma 53:17) [a people who] did not fear death; and they did think more upon the liberty of their fathers than they did upon their lives..." (Alma 56:47)

There will come a time among the Zion people whom the Latter-day Lamanites will lead, when *the strength of the Lord* will be the fear of all nations. For, in obedience to eternal principle reiterated by Washington:

> "...it shall be said among the wicked: Let us not go up to battle against Zion, for the inhabitants of Zion are terrible; wherefore we cannot stand... and it [Zion] shall be the only people that shall not be at war one with another. " (see D&C 45:60-70)

The Purpose of the Book of Mormon's Recordings of Wars

Although Eighty-five instances of armed conflict can be identified in the Book of Mormon (Ricks and Hamblin, *Warfare in the Book of Mormon*, pp. 463-74), various opinions are replete with similarities in regards to Mormon's decision to include detailed narratives about repeated sequences of war, war strategy, and military conflict. Many wonder, "Of all holy writ, why is that in there?"

To mention a few examples, in a critique of Ricks and Hamblin's "Warfare in the Book of Mormon", it's recorded by the Neal A. Maxwell Institute for Religious Scholarship that:

> "Any reader of the Book of Mormon will recall the seemingly endless accounts of marches and countermarches. *They may be boring to many*, but they reflect the realities of maintaining ancient armies." (William J. Hamblin)

Marcus H. Martin's online lecture notes at BYU-Hawaii include the following excerpt:

> "The next 19 chapters in the Book of Alma deal largely with a long and violent war between the Nephites and the Lamanites. Many first-time readers of the Book of Mormon—especially recent converts—have a hard time reading these chapters; in fact, many readers skip them altogether." (http://faculty.byuh.edu/martinsm/Rel 122/Cn122/C22_a43.htm)

Hugh Nibley's summary of "Lecture 65: Alma 48" at the Neil A. Maxwell's Institute for Religious Scholarship records:

"Now we have chapter 48. Do you think this is going to be a letdown? This is on another subject, and it's a "dilly." It's on war. Why do we have to bother about that? We're beyond that sort of barbarism today, aren't we?... The readers of the Book of Mormon are sometimes disgusted with all this... We have always been inclined to rush through the military parts of the Book of Mormon as painful reminders of an unpleasant past. I have studiously ignored the war stories myself. "We'll skip the wars," I said. Alas, if we only could. The whole point of Alma's (or rather Mormon's) studies in the "work of death," as he calls it, is that they are supposed to be revolting—they are meant to be painful. It is Mormon and Moroni, the tragic survivors of a nation destroyed by senseless war, who are editing this book.

"The Book of Mormon is about as negative as you [can] get, isn't it? Well, there must be some reason for that. Don't you get the hint? Why do you think people don't like to read the Book of Mormon? Why do you think we rush through it? We take speed reading courses so it won't slow us down, or else we pick our way through it daintily as through a mine field, avoiding all the unpleasant passages of which there are plenty."

And then Hugh Nibley gives us this profound summation:

"They [Mormon and Moroni] are editing this book, and they have put into it whatever they think might be useful as warning to us. It's not their purpose to tell an entertaining or reassuring tale. War is anything but glamorous in the Book of Mormon. The campaigns and battles are described not as a writer of fiction would depict ancient warfare with all its excitement and color. (Like somebody writing in early New England. That would be popular. Mark Twain or somebody would write about it.) No, it is not what an author in America in the 1820s would imagine as the gaudy trappings of heroic derring-do. That's all missing. It is real war that we see here, a tedious, sordid, plodding, joyless routine of see-saw successes and losses—brutally expensive, destructive, exhausting, and boring, with constant marches and countermarches that end sometimes in fiasco and sometimes in intensely unpleasant engagements. The author writes as one would write—as only one could write—who had gone through a long war as a front-line observer with his eyes wide open. Everything is strictly authentic, with the proper emphasis in the proper place. Strategy and tactics are treated with the knowledge of an expert: logistics and supply; armaments and fortifications; recruiting and training; problems of morale and support from the home front; military intelligence from cloak and dagger to scouting and patrolling; interrogation, guarding, feeding, and exchange of war prisoners; propaganda and psychological warfare; rehabilitation and resettlement; (all these things are there and treated deftly and explicitly); feelers for peace and negotiations at various levels;

treason; profiteering; and the exploitation of the war economy by individuals and groups—it is all there." (http://maxwellinstitute.byu.edu/publications/books/?bookid=118&chapid=1385)

Who was Mormon?

The word "Mormon" means various things to various people. To many, *Mormons* are a group of religious cultists. Then there's the nickname "Mormon" to describe members of the Church of Jesus Christ of Latter-day Saints. There's also the Book of Mormon. But who was Mormon *the person*? Who was this man whom the Lord called upon to serve as the principle abridger of many hundreds of plate records, condensing innumerable writings into this final text? And what was his life like?

When Mormon was 10 years old, Ammaron, who had been keeping and preserving the sacred records, was "constrained by the Holy Ghost [to] hide up the records which were sacred..." (4th Nephi 1:48). It was at this time when he came to the lad for a chat:

> I perceive that thou art a sober child, and art quick to observe; Therefore, when ye are about twenty and four years old I would that ye should remember the things that ye have observed concerning this people; and when ye are of that age go to the land Antum, unto a hill which shall be called Shim; and there have I deposited unto the Lord all the sacred engravings concerning this people. And behold, ye shall take the plates of Nephi unto yourself, and the remainder shall ye leave in the place where they are; and ye shall engrave on the plates of Nephi all the things that ye have observed concerning this people. (Mormon 1:2-4)

At fifteen years of age Mormon was "visited of the Lord, and tasted and knew the goodness of Jesus." (Mormon 1:15) At this point, one would have thought that Mormon may go on to live a life of preaching and prophesying as did Alma, Amulek, Ammon, Nephi, Samuel the Lamanite, and many other Book of Mormon missionaries. But this wasn't his calling. Mormon says:

> And I did endeavor to preach unto this people, but my mouth was shut, and I was forbidden that I should preach unto them; for behold they had wilfully rebelled against their God; and the beloved disciples were taken away out of the land, because of their iniquity. (Mormon 1:16)

Then what *was* Mormon's calling?

> And it came to pass in that same year there began to be a war again between the Nephites and the Lamanites. And notwithstanding I being young, was large in stature; therefore the people of Nephi appointed me that I should be their leader, or the leader of their armies. Therefore it came to pass that in my sixteenth year I did go forth at the head of an army of the Nephites..." (Mormon 2:1-2)

Mormon's life's calling was that of a military leader over a wicked army with perhaps millions of soldiers among their ranks; millions that he would behold, through a lifetime of war, whittled down to just he and twenty-three others before his final departure from the scriptural record. As such, Mormon was to be an observer of brutal death, carnage, rape, and human sacrifice for the entire duration of his long life. Not in all of scripture has there been the record of a righteous man, a prophet of God, at the head of a wicked army. Likewise there has been few, if any, who, almost from birth through old age, have witnessed a greater continual scene of bloodshed and destruction as witnessed by Mormon. For it's recorded that:

> ...notwithstanding the great destruction which hung over my people, they did not repent of their evil doings; therefore there was blood and carnage spread throughout all the face of the land... I... forbear to make a full account of their wickedness and abominations, for behold, a continual scene of wickedness and abominations has been before mine eyes *ever since I have been sufficient to behold the ways of man*. (Mormon 2:8,18)

> And it is impossible for the tongue to describe, or for man to write a perfect description of the horrible scene of the blood and carnage which was among the people, both of the Nephites and of the Lamanites; and every heart was

> hardened, so that they delighted in the shedding of blood continually. (Mormon 4:11)

Then, in his waning years, Mormon gives the following summation of the last struggle of his people:

> And now I finish my record concerning the destruction of my people, the Nephites... I, Mormon, wrote an epistle unto the king of the Lamanites, and desired of him that he would grant unto us that we might gather together our people unto the land of Cumorah, by a hill which was called Cumorah... And it came to pass that the king of the Lamanites did grant unto me the thing which I desired... [and so we] gathered in all the remainder of our people unto the land of Cumorah.
>
> And... behold I, Mormon, began to be old; and [I knew] it to be the last struggle of my people... (Mormon 6:1-6)

The remainder of the chapter describes the day of the "last struggle of my people" as two-hundred and thirty thousand Nephites were hewn down. When this happened, Mormon's soul was "rent with anguish." Lamenting, he looked over the sea of dead carcasses that were once his beloved countrymen and cried:

> O ye fair ones, how could ye have departed from the ways of the Lord! O ye fair ones, how could ye have rejected that Jesus, who stood with open arms to receive you! Behold, if ye had not done this, ye would not have fallen. But behold, ye are fallen, and I mourn your loss. O ye fair sons and daughters, ye fathers and mothers, ye husbands and wives, ye fair ones, how is it that ye could have fallen! But behold, ye are gone, and my sorrows cannot bring your return... O that ye had repented before this great destruction had come upon you. But behold, ye are gone...

This was Mormon. This was the person our all-wise creator chose to bring to millions in our day—*The Book of Mormon.* Mormon *chose* these sections on war so that we would come to an understanding of God's ethics in War—principles that govern 1) entering, 2) combating, and 3) exiting these conflicts. Times of war are NOT times of anarchy. God will hold each of his children individually accountable for every act pertaining to injuring or killing His other children.

Consider King David, a man after God's own heart (1 Sam 13:14). Much like Mormon, King David was a man of war, fighting for Israel in dozens of battles. One can only speculate on how many hundreds or thousands of souls King David killed. God's confidence and approval of King David was secure throughout all these wars. Yet it was when King David intentionally caused the death of an innocent man, Uriah, that he fell from his exaltation (see D&C 132:39).

God's inspiration to Mormon was not an accident, and Mormon included the many war stories into the record of the Book of Mormon for an awesome reason. An all-wise, all knowing, and all-foreseeing God raised up unto Him a servant—Mormon, a man who would have special insight into the horrors of the absolute worst to which mankind can descend, all the while knowing that the extinction of his people could have been avoided.

Are War Stories Actual Scripture?

In the weeks and months contemplating this author's writing of this book, I listened to, during Church Fast and Testimony meeting, a young teenage girl whose testimony included that of expressing a then-recent personal experience in which she was looking for guidance. She opened the Book of Mormon to a random page one night in her bedroom, and mentioned:

> "...it opened up to one of the war sections, and so I thought *there's no inspiration for me in that.*"

Unfortunately, many *adult* members of the church share these sentiments. The war sections of the Book of Mormon are related to the Freedom battle, which today is thought to be a subject separate or unrelated to the gospel. Forty-five years ago, Ezra Taft Benson stated otherwise:

> "Do we preach what governments should *or should not do* as a part of the gospel plan... or do we refuse to follow the [then] Prophet by preaching a limited gospel plan of salvation? The fight for freedom *cannot be divorced from the gospel* – the plan of salvation." (*Our Immediate Responsibility*, BYU Devotional, October 25, 1966)

Years ago, while on an LDS mission in Cincinnati, Ohio, this author's companion responded to the concerns of an investigator struggling with his faith in the Book of Mormon. This particular investigator pointed out a few scriptural references that was the topic of his concern, and was rather critical. Elder Bass' reply was acute and distinctive:

> "Proper investigation of the Book of Mormon involves a submission to its essence and principles, in an effort to discover if the book is true. Yet ultimately, we don't read the book in an effort to constantly find errors and imperfections in its text. We read the Book of Mormon to discover if there are errors and imperfections in *ourselves*."

As reiterated by Hugh Nibley, God leaves nothing to chance. His work is perfect, and His inspiration to the abridgers of the Book of Mormon is without flaw. What is in the Book is *exactly* what the Lord wanted in the Book. The "learned," or those that nitpick its contents will forever be shielded from the beauty, majesty, and truth of this perfect book of war-principles AND Freedom-principles. For:

Wherefore it shall come to pass, that the Lord God will deliver again the book [of Mormon] and the words thereof to him that is *not learned*; and the man *that is not learned* shall say: I am not learned.

Then shall the Lord God say unto him: The learned shall not read them, *for they have rejected them*, and I am able to do mine own work; wherefore thou shalt read the words which I shall give unto thee. (2 Nephi 27:19-20)

War is Victory to Satan

"For verily, verily I say unto you, he that hath the spirit of contention is not of me, but is of the devil, who is the father of contention, and he stirreth up the hearts of men to contend with anger, one with another." (3 Nephi 11:29)

For the Lord worketh not in secret combinations, *neither doth he will that man should shed blood*, but in all things

> hath forbidden it, from the beginning
> of man. (Ether 8:19)

War is victory to Satan. He is the author of death, and it's to his ultimate purpose to cause and promote misery, death, heartache, weeping and regret. In war, no matter which side wins, Satan's purposes are accomplished.

In modern times, war has been a source of confusion to both observers, and those directly involved. Many question whether it's more patriotic to engage in war, or to refrain. Many see preemptive war as a necessary evil, and the way of ultimate self-protection. Considering the wars of this and the last century, a neutral observer may wonder and repeatedly ask the question, "Now, what exactly was our country trying to accomplish?"

Then there are covert reasons for war. Ranks of soldiers are told not to question superior officer's orders, even if it costs them their lives and the lives of many others. This principle of obeying orders at all costs is incorrect, according to Sun Tzu in his original *The Art of War*, which states:

> "There are roads which must not be
> followed, armies which must not be

> attacked, towns which must not be besieged, positions which must not be contested, and *commands of the sovereign which must not be obeyed."* (Sun Tzu VIII:3)

And:

> *If fighting is sure to result in victory, then you must fight, even though the ruler forbid it; if fighting will not result in victory, then you must not fight even at the ruler's bidding.* (Sun Tzu X:23)

Following this principle, even Teancum used common sense to disobey the orders of Captain Moroni as recorded in Alma. (see Alma 52:16-17)

Ezra Taft Benson pointed out that during the War in Vietnam U.S. soldiers were sometimes being fired upon for 2 ½ hours before superior officers would authorize return fire. (*Our Immediate Responsibility, BYU Devotional, October 25, 1966*) How is this helpful to a country trying to win a war? Are not commanding officers who restrain their soldiers from defending themselves, themselves murderers? It is these and other types of incredible orders which had Elder Benson conclude, as one of his "10 Occurrences which Aid the Enemies of Freedom":

> "...by the sacrifice of American manhood by engaging in wars we apparently have no intention of winning." (*Our Immediate Responsibility*)

Such has been the frustration of wars dating back a century and a half, or longer. Gadianton Robbers, those who would use war for profit and control, have long since taken the reigns of leadership. They stir the people up under a false pretense—of which there are numerous examples of in The Book of Mormon (for example Alma 48:1-3, Alma 54:23-24—55:1, 3 Nephi 3:9-10), while using those who depend on them for leadership to do their dark bidding.

Concerning these robbers, Elder John A. Widtsoe has said:

> "The Gadianton Robbers from the Book of Mormon are loose among us. The King-men, and women, are running our government. And, worst of all, we are blindly electing them, or appointing them so they can continue to destroy the things we cherish most... Men of false principles have preyed upon us like wolves upon helpless lambs." — (Conference Report, April 1944)

And Elder Ezra Taft Benson stated:

> "Now undoubtedly Moroni could have pointed out many factors that led to the destruction of the people, but notice how he singled out the secret combinations, just as the Church today could point out many threats to peace, prosperity, and the spread of God's work, but it has singled out the greatest threat as the godless conspiracy. *There is no conspiracy theory in the Book of Mormon—it is a conspiracy fact.*" (Civic Standards for the Faithful Saints, July 1972 Ensign Report)

Despite many genuine actions of heroism among soldiery, because of those who lead these efforts—and their evil intent—wars of our era have been modeled after the final series of wars in the Book of Mormon in that the wicked have warred against the wicked. Mormon gives this summation of his own experience:

> "And... they did come down again to battle. And we did beat them again, and did slay a great number of them... And now, because of this great thing which my people, the Nephites, had

done, they began to boast in their own strength, and began to swear before the heavens that they would avenge themselves of the blood of their brethren... that they would go up to battle against their enemies, and would cut them off from the face of the land. And it came to pass that I, Mormon, did utterly refuse from this time forth to be a commander and a leader of this people, because of their wickedness and abomination." (Mormon 3:6-11)

And so what was the result?

"And now it came to pass that... the Nephites did go up with their armies to battle against the Lamanites... And it came to pass that the armies of the Nephites were driven back again to the land of Desolation. And while they were yet weary, a fresh army of the Lamanites did come upon them; and they had a sore battle, insomuch that the Lamanites did take possession of the city Desolation, and did slay many of the Nephites, and did take many prisoners... And it was because the armies of the Nephites went up unto

> the Lamanites that they began to be smitten; for were it not for that, the Lamanites could have had no power over them. *But, behold, the judgments of God will overtake the wicked; and **it is by the wicked that the wicked are punished; for it is the wicked that stir up the hearts of the children of men unto bloodshed.*** " (Mormon 4:1-5)

In this example, the leadership ON BOTH SIDES who did "stir up the hearts of the children of men unto bloodshed" was in stark contrast to the majority of the wars in the Book of Mormon, where a definitive good fought a definitive evil. Consider the following:

> "Now the chiefest among all the chief captains and the great commander of all the armies of the Nephites was appointed, and his name was Gidgiddoni. *Now it was the custom among all the Nephites to appoint for their chief captains, (save it were in their times of wickedness) some one that had the spirit of revelation and also prophecy; therefore, this Gidgiddoni was a great prophet among them.*" (3 Nephi 3:17-18)

In the Book of Mormon leaders of righteous armies were BOTH "chief captains of the armies" and "prophets". The results of such leadership ALWAYS ended victorious for those on the Lord's side. This is the remarkable 1st principle of the Book of Mormon's *Art of War* (shown later). In the particular story of Chief Captain Gidgiddoni, once again, peace was restored:

> "And now it was Gidgiddoni, and the judge, Lachoneus, and those who had been appointed leaders, who had established this great peace in the land." (3 Nephi 6:6)

But again, today's wars are not fought according to Book of Mormon *Art of War* principles. It is NOT our custom to appoint for our chief captains those that have the "spirit of revelation and also prophecy." How can a faithful member of this church have any faith in the leadership of Gadianton Robbers, who stir us up, then send us out? In fact, the only war in history's last millennia that resembles the majority of wars in the Book of Mormon was the United States War of Independence—a war prophesied of, in detail, in the Book of Mormon record itself (see 1 Nephi 13).

Today, many LDS Americans think that the United States is on the right side of every issue when our troops are sent out to fight, but how can this possibly be the case?

In his Farewell Address, George Washington said, "It is our true policy to steer clear of permanent alliances with any portion of the foreign world." (George Washington, Presidential Farewell Address, September 17, 1796) And likewise Thomas Jefferson said, "Commerce with all nations, alliance with none, should be our motto." (Thomas Jefferson, LETTER CCLII.—TO T. LOMAX, March 12, 1799)

Given these statements, along with the mandate of Jesus himself in the Sermon on the Mount found in Matthew 5, it's apparent to this author that the United States hasn't been on the complete right side of ANY foreign war since the days of our Founders! Yet how much blood have these wars shed, and how many lives have these wars taken?

The apostle John mentioned that the Devil, that old serpent, "deceiveth the whole world." (Revelations 12:9)

In a landmark 1986 conference address, Ezra Taft Benson stated that the Book of Mormon mirrors our day. Said he:

> "The second great reason why we must make the Book of Mormon a center

focus of study is that it was written for our day. The Nephites never had the book; neither did the Lamanites of ancient times. It was meant for us... Each of the major writers of the Book of Mormon testified that he wrote for future generations... Mormon himself said, "Yea, I speak unto you, ye remnant of the house of Israel" (Mormon 7:1). And Moroni, the last of the inspired writers, actually saw our day and time. "Behold," he said, "the Lord hath shown unto me great and marvelous things concerning that which must shortly come, at that day when these things shall come forth among you.

"Behold, I speak unto you as if ye were present, and yet ye are not. But behold, Jesus Christ hath shown you unto me, and I know your doing." (Mormon 8:34–35)

"By careful study of that time period, we can determine why some were destroyed in the terrible judgments that preceded His coming and what brought others to stand at the temple in the land of Bountiful and thrust their hands into the wounds of His hands and feet.

"From the Book of Mormon we learn how disciples of Christ live in times of war. From the Book of Mormon we see the evils of secret combinations portrayed in graphic and chilling reality..." (The Book of Mormon, Keystone of our Religion, Conference Report, 1986)

A year later, President Benson further remarked:

"Recently I have been reading again the marvelous account in the Book of Mormon of the visit of the resurrected Savior to the American continent. As Easter approaches, I have been deeply impressed with the beauty and power of this scriptural account in 3 Nephi, and with its great value for our time and our generation.

"The record of the Nephite history just prior to the Savior's visit reveals many parallels to our own day as we anticipate the Savior's second coming.

The Nephite civilization had reached great heights. They were prosperous and industrious. They had built many cities with great highways connecting them. They engaged in shipping and trade. They built temples and palaces.

"But, as so often happens, the people rejected the Lord. Pride became commonplace. Dishonesty and immorality were widespread. Secret combinations flourished because, as Helaman tells us, the Gadianton robbers "had seduced the more part of the righteous until they had come down to believe in their works and partake of their spoils." (Helaman 6:38) "The people began to be distinguished by ranks, according to their riches and their chances for learning." (3 Nephi 6:12) And "Satan had great power, unto the stirring up of the people to do all manner of iniquity, and to the puffing them up with pride, tempting them to seek for power, and authority, and riches, and the vain things of the world," even as today." (3 Nephi 6:15)

In God's wisdom, in providing a book that would go forth in our day through the Prophet Joseph Smith, a "Keystone of our Religion", the "…most correct of any book on earth", and a book in which "man would get nearer to God by abiding by its precepts, than by any other book" (History of the Church, 4:461), He has included a record in which on almost every turn, good is contesting with evil in wars, written in great description.

The Book of Mormon is primarily NOT a book in which the wicked war against the wicked, as in our day. It's a book which records Satan's influence physically contending to bloodshed those who have garnered *the strength of the Lord.* Can we not expect this *strength* to be restored? Can we not expect holy prophets to be leaders of armies? Should we not expect the day will come when godly principles of war will be put into action as part of the restoration of all things in the last days (found in D&C 86:10 and 27:6)? Is this not why the Lord chose to include these principles in the Book of Mormon, so that godly military leaders who also have the spirit of prophecy and revelation will lead, once again, according to principles of truth and righteousness?

> "Wherefore, O ye Gentiles, it is wisdom in God that these things should be shown unto you, that thereby ye may

repent of your sins, and suffer not that these murderous combinations shall get above you, which are built up to get power and gain—and the work, yea, even the work of destruction come upon you, yea, even the sword of the justice of the Eternal God shall fall upon you, to your overthrow and destruction if ye shall suffer these things to be.

"Wherefore, the Lord commandeth you, when ye shall see these things come among you that ye shall awake to a sense of your awful situation, because of this secret combination which shall be among you; or wo be unto it, because of the blood of them who have been slain; for they cry from the dust for vengeance upon it, and also upon those who built it up.

"For it cometh to pass that whoso buildeth it up seeketh to overthrow the freedom of all lands, nations, and countries; and it bringeth to pass the destruction of all people, for it is built up by the devil..." (Ether 8:23-25)

Should NOT God raise up leaders to Himself who will contend with these forewarned murderers with their planned atrocities, in the re-establishment of freedom? And should not these leaders be firm in the understanding of what it means to go out *in the strength of the Lord*? Or, in other words, should these leaders not be well acquainted with God's version of *Art of War* principles?

This author is resolved to believe that we will soon see a time when the righteous will be called again to go out *in the strength of the Lord*—a phrase that appears thirty times in various forms in Book of Mormon scripture.

Sun Tzu's Art of War

The original *Art of War* is an ancient Chinese military treatise that is attributed to Sun Tzu, a high ranking military general and strategist during the late Spring and Autumn period (around 600 BC). It is composed of 13 chapters, each of which is devoted to one aspect of warfare. It is the definitive work on military strategies and tactics, and is aptly read for its military insight. Author Ralph Sawyer has remarked, "…for the last two thousand years it [Sun Tzu's *Art of War*] has remained the most important military treatise in Asia, where even the common people know it by name." (Sawyer, Ralph D. The Seven Military Classics of Ancient China. New York: Basic Books. 2007. p. 149)

To say that Sun Tzu has had an influence on worldwide military thinking would be an understatement. Simply, the *Art of War* is the most widely reproduced and circulated military text in the history of the world, in and outside of Asia.

There are one-to-one parallels with Sun Tzu principles and the *Art of War* principles found in the Book of Mormon. For example, Sun Tzu says "All warfare is based on deception" (Sun Tzu I:18), "Hold out baits to entice the enemy" (Sun Tzu I:20), and "If your opponent is of choleric temper, seek to irritate him." (Sun Tzu I:22)

The Book of Mormon's Art of War seeks to interweave eternal principles for victory in war taught by Sun Tzu with additional principles taught by the Lord and His prophets as revealed in the Book of Mormon. Hence this work is an addition or appendage to Sun Tzu's wisdom with the important ingredient of revelation through a work that is considered *the most correct of any book on earth*, and which Gordon B. Hinckley has said:

> ...in its [The Book of Mormon's] descriptions of the problems of today's society, it is as current as the morning newspaper and much more definitive, inspired, and inspiring concerning the solutions of those problems... (*A Testimony Vibrant and True,*" Ensign, August 2005)

It is acknowledged that additional insight could be elaborated upon using the Bible, and particularly the battle stories of Israel in the Old Testament. However, the primary resources for this work have been two sources—Sun Tzu's *Art of War*, and the Book of Mormon.

A Word about the Enemy

Our enemies are real. When you are tempted to sin, it isn't a random thought that found its way to your mind, like the role of a dice that comes up snake eyes. It is Satan and his hierarchy of 1/3 of the hosts of heaven in action, deliberately DOING what their master has told them to do. Temptations are whispers of wicked spirit's mouths into your spiritual ears. They are suggestions which, if allowed to continue, will grow stronger and stronger until the day comes when your liberty to resist is taken from you, and you are helplessly led by the evil one—that being for which you have chosen to follow over and over again:

> For behold, if ye have procrastinated the day of your repentance even until death, behold, ye have become subjected to the spirit of the devil, and he doth seal you his; therefore, the Spirit of the Lord hath withdrawn from you, and hath no place in you, and the devil hath all power over you; and this is the final state of the wicked. (Alma 34:35)

But you need NOT become subject to his power. You are a child of God. Satan and his minions are NOT God's children. As such, he has the power to **bruise** your heal, while you have the power to **crush** his head (Genesis 3:15, GOD's WORD translation©).

To accomplish his design, Satan follows the same *Art of War* principles as Sun Tzu would admonish, minus a few principles where Sun Tzu includes a token from On High, such as the principle:

> *The general who advances without coveting fame and retreats without fearing disgrace, whose only thought is to protect his country and do good service for his sovereign, is the jewel of the kingdom.* (Sun Tzu X:24)

Since secular principles are all Satan has to work with, being in direct opposition to additional strength which comes from God, he is left to these resources *ONLY*. Hence the difference between Sun Tzu's secular *Art of War*, and the Book of Mormon's *Art of War* is the difference between *bruising one's heal*, and *crushing one's head*.

Nephi said:

> "For we labor diligently... to persuade our children, and also our brethren, to believe in Christ, and to be reconciled to God; for we know that it is by <u>grace</u> that we are saved, <u>*after all we can do*</u>." (2 Nephi 25:23)

Sun Tzu's masterpiece is of great value, and SHOULD be included as a foundational base for strategy, *but adding the additional principles that are contained in the Book of Mormon ensures victory*—for how can God *ever* fail? Studying Sun Tzu's *Art of War* is "all we can do", while "grace" is what God can and will do should we have faith in Him and be worthy of His omniscient and omnipotent intervention.

Sun Tzu's principles of the *Art of War* can be likened to the strategy of a grandmaster Chess player whose predictive foresight is unsurpassed to other men, while the Book of Mormon's principles in the *Art of War* illustrates weak man's strategy and strength, however brilliant, contending with God's. Book of Mormon *Art of War* principles enables God to hold the sword for which weak man charges into battle with. It enables man's clarity to be that of God's perfect understanding and infinite knowledge—a glorified being who "measure[s] the waters in the hollow of his hand... comprehend[s] the dust of the earth... weigh[s] the mountains in scales, and the hills in a balance.... [wherefore] the nations [are] as a drop of a bucket, and are counted as the small dust of the balance." (see Isaiah 40:12-15).

Zeniff contrasts his armies, which went out "In the Strength of the Lord" for reasons of strictly defense, with the logic the Lamanites used for going to battle. He explains:

> They [the Lamanites] were a wild, and ferocious, and a blood-thirsty people, believing in the tradition of their

fathers, which is this—**Believing that they were driven out of the land of Jerusalem because of the iniquities of their fathers**, and that they were wronged in the wilderness by their brethren, and they were also wronged while crossing the sea;

And again, that they were **wronged while in the land of their first inheritance**, after they had crossed the sea, and all this because that Nephi was more faithful in keeping the commandments of the Lord—therefore he was favored of the Lord, for the Lord heard his prayers and answered them, and he took the lead of their journey in the wilderness.

And his brethren were wroth with him because they understood not the dealings of the Lord; they were also **wroth with him upon the waters** because they hardened their hearts against the Lord.

And again, they were **wroth with him when they had arrived in the promised land, because they said that**

> **he had taken the ruling of the people** out of their hands; and they sought to kill him.
>
> And again, they were wroth with him because he departed into the wilderness as the Lord had commanded him, and took the [holy] records which were engraven on the plates of brass, **for they said that he robbed them.** (Mosiah 10:12-16)

Because of these gaping differences of *ability*, you might say that Satan, in all his illogic, has become an expert in what he has to work with—the strength of man (rather than God). In other words, Satan has become an expert in Sun Tzu's *Art of War*. Sun Tzu says:

> "*All warfare is based on deception.* Hence, when we are able to attack, we must seem unable; when using our forces, we must appear inactive; when we are near, we must make the enemy believe we are far away; when far away, we must make him believe we are near." (Sun Tzu I:18-19)

Yet does the Lord use these tactics as well?

Indeed these tactics resemble that of Satan, that old serpent? But does this seem to be the way in which God works—through lies, misdirection, and deceit?

The first answer is NO:

> "For behold, my beloved brethren, I say unto you that the Lord God worketh not in darkness." (2 Nephi 26:23)

Yet, in preserving the light of life, liberty, property, "...our God, our religion, and freedom, and our peace, our wives, and our children" (Alma 26:12) the darkest of acts are justified. God's paramount hope for His righteous children is that they have the insight to understand the difference between the cold-blooded murders of his misguided children, and shedding blood in defense of all that mankind holds dear. In the Book of Mormon, righteous armies use deception, lies, and misdirection, as taught by Sun Tzu a half a world away during the same era.

To borrow a line from the movie *V for Vendetta,* God's servants sometimes "use lies to tell the truth, while politicians [Satan] use them to cover the truth up."

The Philosophies of Tao Te Ching

The philosophies of Tao Te Ching apply. Tao Te Ching means "the Way of life." The philosophies described within the Tao Te Ching provide the foundation of the Taoist religion and the Taoist philosophy prominent in China during Sun Tzu's time.

The phrase "the journey of a thousand miles begins with a single step," commonly used in both the East and West, is from the Tao Te Ching. It communicates the humble origins of even the greatest endeavors.

Like the scriptures, the Tao Te Ching acknowledges that a state's leadership cannot always avoid war. Lao Tzu therefore believed a military triumph should be treated as a funeral simply because war proved necessary at all. Sun Tzu, like any soldier trying to reconcile his religion with war, would have benefited from Lao Tzu's words, who said:

> Arms, however beautiful, are instruments of ill omen, hateful to all creatures. Those who know the way of life do not wish to employ them. *The superior man prefers his higher nature, but in time of war, will call upon his lower nature.* Weapons are an

> instrument of ill omen, and not the instruments of the superior man, until he has no choice but to employ them. Peace is what he prizes; victory through forces of arms is to him undesirable. To consider armed victory desirable would be to delight in killing men, and he who delights in killing men will not prevail on the world. To celebrate when man's higher nature comes forth is the prized position; when his lower nature comes forth is time for mourning.
>
> ...He who has killed multitudes of men should weep for them; and the victor in battle has his place accorded as in a funeral. (from *The Art of War*, by Robert L. Cantrell, p. 3-4)

Does this not sound like Moroni of the Book of Mormon, and his armies?

> And Moroni was a strong and a mighty man; he was a man of a perfect understanding; yea, a man that did not delight in bloodshed; a man whose soul did joy in the liberty and the freedom

of his country, and his brethren from bondage and slavery…

…and they [Moroni's armies] were also taught never to give an offense, yea, and never to raise the sword except it were against an enemy, except it were to preserve their lives…

Now, they [Moroni's armies] were sorry to take up arms against the Lamanites, because they did not delight in the shedding of blood; yea, and this was not all—they were sorry to be the means of sending so many of their brethren out of this world into an eternal world, unprepared to meet their God. (Alma 48:11-16, 23)

The Acme of Skill: Understanding, Diffusing, Conquering

"My people are destroyed for lack of knowledge." (Hosea 4:6)

Another of Sun Tzu's *Art of War* principles is:

> "For to win one hundred victories in one hundred battles is not the acme of skill. To subdue the enemy *without fighting* is the acme of skill." (Sun Tzu III:2)

This is the victory God's disciples pursue; but judging from history, and especially when judging from Book of Mormon history, such a strategy for victory is NOT what can be expected.

To "*subdue the enemy without fighting*" is also the victory *our enemies* pursue with every intent to win, WITHOUT force of arms. Although it is not the intent of this book to educate, and "awake[n] [you] to a sense of your awful situation," (Ether 8:24) suffice it to say that, from the words of a great patriot:

> "Today, there is a great threat to freedom. The Church is prospering and growing, but all over the world the light of freedom is being diminished. A great struggle for the minds of men is now being waged. At issue is whether or not man's basic inalienable rights of life, liberty, property, and pursuit of happiness shall be recognized. It is the same struggle over which the war in heaven was waged. In undiminished

fury, and with an anxiety that his time is short—and it is—the great adversary to all men is attempting to destroy man's freedom and to see him totally subjugated... [with] no regard for human life." (Ezra Taft Benson, *This Nation Shall Endure*, p. 5)

And from an enslaver's vantage point:

"Gradually, by selective breeding, the congenital differences between rulers and ruled will increase until they become almost different species. A revolt [war] of the plebs ["The People"] would become as unthinkable as an organized insurrection of sheep against the practice of eating mutton." (Bertrand Russell, *The Impact of Science on Society*)

Resisting forces that would enslave us and destroy our freedoms is not easy work. It wasn't easy in the Book of Mormon. It wasn't easy when our Forefathers founded this country. It's not going to be easy today.

Said Thomas Paine:

"Tyranny, like hell, is not easily conquered; yet we have this consolation with us, that the harder the conflict, the more glorious the triumph. What we obtain too cheap, we esteem too lightly: it is dearness only that gives every thing its value. Heaven knows how to put a proper price upon its goods; and it would be strange indeed if so celestial an article as FREEDOM should not be highly rated." (The Crisis, 1776)

And from J. Reuben Clark:

"...one constitutional right after another [is being] yielded without any real contest, [and] our backs [are] getting nearer to the wall with each retreat. It is now proposed we retreat still further. Is not this suicide? Is there anyone so naive as to think that things will right themselves without a fight? There has been no more fight in us than there is in a bunch of sheep, and we have been much like sheep. Freedom was never brought to a people on a silver platter, nor maintained with whisk brooms and lavender sprays.... The whole course is deliberately planned and carried out, its purpose is to destroy the Constitution and our constitutional government; then to bring chaos out of which the new Statism, with its Slavery, is to arise, with a cruel, relentless, selfish, ambitious crew in the saddle, riding hard with whip and spur, a red-shrouded band of night riders for despotism." (Church News, September 25, **1959**, Pg. 327-328)

"I say to you that the price of liberty is and always has been blood, human blood, and if our liberties are lost, we shall never regain them except at the price of blood." (Church News, November 20, 1952, Pg. 71)

For this reason this book is spawned, as a call for the godly armies of the Book of Mormon to organize once again in defense of our liberty, "...our God, our religion, and freedom, and our peace, our wives, and our children." (Alma 26:12).

As in the Declaration of Independence:

"Prudence, indeed, will dictate that Governments long established should not be changed for light and transient

> causes; and accordingly all experience hath shewn that mankind are more disposed to suffer, while evils are sufferable than to right themselves by abolishing the forms to which they are accustomed. *But when a long train of abuses and usurpations, pursuing invariably the same Object evinces a design to reduce them under absolute Despotism, it is their right, it is their duty, to throw off such Government, and to provide new Guards for their future security."*

Although we must never give up petitioning government to act within the bounds of the Constitution, the time for finding solutions with a pen are speedily yielding to those which can only be obtained by the sword. (see Alma 61:14)

As Thomas Jefferson aptly said:

> "The tree of liberty must be refreshed from time to time with the blood of patriots and tyrants. It is its natural manure." (Thomas Jefferson to William Stephens Smith, Paris, 13 Nov. 1787)

As godly patriots, let us be ready, willing and able to answer the call, again, of the glorious cause of America.

As I watch the Sun while it sets,
My mind it seems doth flee.
I think of my Nation's regrets,
And a Country which shouldn't be.

The experiment began long ago,
When humble men stood tall.
God's wisdom from them did flow,
As they answered liberty's call.

Redeeming this glorious land,
Came by the shedding of Patriot's blood,
Who were aware of God's mighty hand,
While stomping through frozen mud.

A foundation successfully laid,
As Ben Franklin, signing, did weep.
Then when asked, "What system was made?"
Said he, "A Republic, if it you can keep!"

So I look at the setting Sun,
Imagining Ben NOT proud,
Having left their intent undone,
Dead voices cry aloud,

"Will you dishonor your forefathers too,
In the foundation we painfully set?"
"Or is there among you a few,
Who will labor and bleed and sweat?"

Said Jefferson, "The blood of Patriots and slavers,
Tis the Liberty Trees' manure."
Will YOU become your fellow man's savers,
In a Nation which shall endure?

Can you clearly hear the call of your country?

The Vital Role of the Latter-day Lamanites

...for pangs have taken thee as a woman in travail. Be in pain, and labour to bring forth, O daughter of Zion, like a woman in travail: for now shalt thou go forth out of the city, and thou shalt dwell in the field, and thou shalt go even to Babylon; there shalt thou be delivered; there the Lord shall redeem thee from the hand of thine enemies.

Now also many nations are gathered against thee, that say, Let her be defiled, and let our eye look upon Zion. But they know not the thoughts of the Lord, neither understand they his counsel: for he shall gather them as the sheaves into the floor.

Arise and thresh, O daughter of Zion: for I will make thine horn iron, and I will make thy hoofs brass: and thou shalt beat in pieces many people...

> And the remnant of Jacob shall be among the Gentiles in the midst of many people as a lion among the beasts of the forest, as a young lion among the flocks of sheep: who, if he go through, both treadeth down, and teareth in pieces, and none can deliver. (Micah 4:9-13, 5:8)
>
> ...
>
> But before the great day of the Lord shall come, Jacob shall flourish in the wilderness, and the Lamanites shall blossom as the rose. (D&C 49:24)

The Latter-day Lamanites are the children of the Book of Mormon peoples. Joseph Smith said the Book of Mormon gave an, "...*account of the former inhabitants of this continent*, and the source from whence they sprang." (JSH 1:34) Furthermore, they are primarily the people for whom the Book of Mormon was written to. Mormon's son Moroni tells us that the:

> "...power to bring it [**the Book of Mormon**] to light... shall be done with an eye single to his [**God's**] glory, *or the welfare of the ancient and long*

> *dispersed covenant people of the Lord* [**the Latter-day Lamanites**]..., [for] we have desired concerning our brethren [**Latter-day Lamanites**], yea, even their restoration to the knowledge of Christ." (Mormon 8:15, 9:36)

The Latter-day Lamanites are primarily the Indians on the American continent, a remnant of the house of Israel with a great destiny to lead the charge of the righteous to a Zion that will be built in Independence, Missouri. Their destiny of not only leading this charge, but protecting its people will come while waving Moroni's Title of Liberty and rallying those who will follow into true and just law, while being uninhibited from warring enemies (to say the least) in their march. All this is according to prophecy.

From Mormon 5:

> ... a knowledge of these things [**in the Book of Mormon**] must come unto the remnant of these people [**Latter-day Lamanites**], and also unto the Gentiles [**mainstream Americans**], who the Lord hath said should scatter this people, and this people should be counted as naught among them—therefore I write a small abridgment, daring not to give a

full account of the things which I have seen, because of the commandment which I have received... And now behold, this I speak unto their seed [**American Indians**], and also to the Gentiles who have care for the house of Israel, that realize and know from whence their blessings come [**mainstream Americans who are converted members of the Church**].

Now these things are written unto the remnant of the house of Jacob [**American Indians**]; and they are written after this manner, because it is known of God that wickedness will not bring them [**the writings of the Book of Mormon**] forth unto them [**American Indians**]; and they are to be hid up unto the Lord that they may come forth in his own due time.

And this is the commandment which I have received; and behold, they [**writings of the Book of Mormon**] shall come forth according to the commandment of the Lord, when he shall see fit, in his wisdom. And behold, they shall go... that... the seed of this people [**American Indians**] may more fully believe his gospel, which shall go forth unto them from the Gentiles [**LDS missionaries and other Saints**]; for this people shall be scattered, and shall become a dark, a filthy, and a loathsome people, beyond the description of that which ever hath been amongst us, yea, even that which hath been among the Lamanites, and this because of their unbelief and idolatry...

They were once a delightsome people, and they had Christ for their shepherd; yea, they were led even by God the Father. But now, behold, they are led about by Satan, even as chaff is driven before the wind, or as a vessel is tossed about upon the waves, without sail or anchor, or without anything wherewith to steer her; and even as she is, so are they.

And behold, the Lord hath reserved their blessings, which they might have received in the land, for the Gentiles who shall possess the land [**of America**].

But behold... after they have been driven and scattered by the Gentiles, behold, then will the Lord remember the covenant which he made unto Abraham and unto all the house of Israel. And also the Lord will remember the prayers of the righteous, which have been put up unto him for them [**American Indians, or Latter-day Lamanites**].

And then, O ye Gentiles [**mainstream America**], how can ye stand before the power of God [**power God will give to the American Indians**], except ye shall repent and turn from your evil ways? Know ye not that ye are in the hands of God? Know ye not that he hath all power, and at his great command the earth shall be rolled together as a scroll? Therefore, repent ye, and humble yourselves before him, lest he shall come out in justice against you— lest a remnant of the seed of Jacob [**American Indians**] shall go forth among you as a lion, and tear you in pieces, and there is none to deliver. (Mormon 5:9-24)

More is spoken about pertaining to Mormon's words in 3 Nephi 16 by Jesus Christ himself, though His words, He perceived, were not being understood. After his explanation to the Latter-day Lamanites' ancestors in 3 Nephi 16 he says:

> Behold, my time is at hand. I perceive that ye are weak, that ye cannot understand all my words which I am commanded of the Father to speak unto you at this time. (3 Nephi 17:1-2)

Although Jesus didn't, at this point, specifically name the Freedom and Liberty portions of His gospel (He does later on), it can be perceived that the principles of liberty are what Jesus was referring to as a "fullness of my gospel", as opposed to His gospel, yet NOT in its fullness.

It's not the intent of this book to point out the reasons why the Church has become silent on the subject of freedom since the early 70's. Suffice it to say that the LDS *membership's* choice of apathy initiated this direction, <u>NOT the Church itself</u>. This is a history that has repeated itself:

> And the Lord said unto Samuel, Hearken unto the voice of the people in all that they say unto thee: for they

have not rejected thee, *but they have rejected me*, that I should not reign over them. (1 Samuel 8:7)

Perhaps the quote below, among the many decades of pleadings, resembles a crux of open doctrine from the brethren during this generation.

The following are the words of Elder Henry D. Moyle, who later served in the First Presidency with J. Reuben Clark and David O. McKay:

> "'Of all the dispositions and habits that lead to political prosperity, religion and morality are indispensable supports' [Moyle quotes from George Washington's Farewell address]. Now listen to that quote from the Father of our Country and ask yourselves, 'Should religion play a role in politics?' [He then quotes Washington's remarks again] Tell me, how are we going to give those supports to political prosperity if we keep our mouths closed concerning political matters? I want to say to you today that just as sure as we live, the only reason that we have become so circumspect in what we say about politics in our religious

> gatherings is because of the influence and the effort that our enemies have made to close our mouths—and don't let anybody fool you on that!
>
> I say that the mouths of our leaders should not be closed and that we should never permit anybody to inculcate in our hearts the idea that we in this church cannot speak concerning matters upon which our independence and our freedom depends." (BYU Devotional, October 10, **1950**, Elder Henry D. Moyle)

(For a much fuller conversation, please read a previous work of the author, "That Ye May Marvel: The 7 Epoch Shifts in Civilization's Destiny," Archive Publishing, 2011)

Jesus States in 3 Nephi 16:

> And because of the mercies of the Father unto the Gentiles, and also the judgments of the Father upon my people who are of the house of Israel [**American Indians**], verily, verily, I say unto you, that after all this, and I have caused my people who are of the

house of Israel [**American Indians**] to be smitten, and to be afflicted, and to be slain, and to be cast out from among them, and to become hated by them, and to become a hiss and a byword among them—...

At that day when the Gentiles [**Church members of every denomination, including LDS**] shall sin against my gospel, and shall reject the fulness of my gospel [**the liberty portion of the gospel**], and shall be lifted up in the pride of their hearts above all nations, and above all the people of the whole earth, and shall be filled with all manner of lyings, and of deceits, and of mischiefs, and all manner of hypocrisy, and murders, and priestcrafts, and whoredoms, and of secret abominations; and if they shall do all those things, and shall reject the *fulness* of my gospel [**the liberty portion**], behold, saith the Father, I will bring the *fulness* of my gospel from among them. (3 Nephi 16:9-10)

Jesus isn't saying that the *gospel* will He bring from among them, but *a fullness of the gospel*. This has happened! The Church has a fullness of the gospel, but its members, the Gentiles, do *not*. We have rejected the liberty portions, and thus a *fullness of the gospel* is not among the Gentiles. Quotes like Elder Moyle's were common among Church leaders, but the membership didn't obey, and so, like the Lord told Samuel of old, "…they [**the Saints**] have not rejected thee, but they have rejected me…." (1 Samuel 8:7).

Yet God has made a provision for the "fulness" to return to the Gentiles, as spoken in the remainder of Jesus' discourse:

> And then will I remember my covenant which I have made unto my people, O house of Israel [**American Indians**], and I will bring my gospel unto them. And I will show unto thee, O house of Israel, that the Gentiles shall not have power over you; but I will remember my covenant unto you, O house of Israel, *and ye shall come unto the knowledge of the fulness of my gospel* [**The American Indians are destined to have and promote the** *entire* **gospel, including the liberty portions of it, perhaps** *especially* **the liberty portions of it**].

But if the Gentiles will repent and return unto me, saith the Father, behold they shall be numbered among my people, O house of Israel. And I will not suffer my people, who are of the house of Israel [**American Indians**], to go through among them, and tread them down, saith the Father.

But if they will not turn unto me, and hearken unto my voice, I will suffer them, yea, I will suffer my people, O house of Israel, that they shall go through among them, and shall tread them down, and they shall be as salt that hath lost its savor, which is thenceforth good for nothing but to be cast out, and to be trodden under foot of my people, O house of Israel.

Verily, verily, I say unto you, thus hath the Father commanded me—that I should give unto this people [**American Indians**] this land for their inheritance. And then the words of the prophet Isaiah shall be fulfilled, which say: Thy watchmen shall lift up the voice; with the voice together shall they sing, for they shall see eye to eye when the Lord shall bring again Zion [**New Jerusalem at Independence, Missouri, and the cause to go to Zion will be the cause to return to liberty, "for out of Zion shall go forth <u>the law</u>...", Isaiah 2:3**]. (3 Nephi 16:11-18)

Zion and *The New Jerusalem* are interchangeable names of the same great city that will be built in Independence, Missouri in the future to which we are quickly advancing. This holy city is also referred to as *The Kingdom of* God, or the place many will go to enjoy a truly free society with its (adhered to) Constitutional government; "for *out of Zion shall go forth the law*, and the word of the Lord from Jerusalem." (Isaiah 2:3)

Most Saints understand bits and pieces about the New Jerusalem, in which God's civil law will bear rule. What fewer Saints know, however, is that this great co-capital of the world will be set up "unto a remnant of the seed of Joseph" (Ether 13:6), or unto the Latter-day Lamanites.

The phrase "remnant of Jacob" in the Book of Mormon refers to the Latter-day Lamanites in certain passages, but *also* refers to the Jews—depending on the verse. However, the phrase "remnant of Joseph," in every instance in the Book of Mormon refers to the posterity of the people that are living at that time, or the Latter-day Lamanites. For example, "And behold, are we not a remnant of the seed of Joseph?" (3 Nephi 10:17) and "Behold, we are a remnant of the seed of Jacob; yea, [**or to be more precise**] we are a remnant of the seed of Joseph, whose coat was rent by his brethren into many pieces." (Alma 46:23; see also Alma 46:23-24, 3 Nephi 5:23, Ether 13)

We are told clearly that the New Jerusalem will be *not unto the Gentiles*, while righteous Gentiles will surely be adopted into the House of Israel, and occupy it. The great city will be unto the Latter-day Lamanites, as explained three separate times in five subsequent scriptures, found in Ether 13:6-10:

> And that a New Jerusalem should be built up upon this land, <u>unto the remnant of the seed of Joseph</u>, for which things there has been a type. For as Joseph brought his father down into the land of Egypt, even so he died there; wherefore, the Lord brought a remnant of the seed of Joseph out of the land of Jerusalem, that he might be merciful unto the seed of Joseph that they should perish not, even as he was merciful unto the father of Joseph that he should perish not.

> *Wherefore, the remnant of the house of Joseph shall be built upon this land*; and it shall be a land of their inheritance; *and they shall build up a holy city* unto the Lord, like unto the Jerusalem of old; and they shall no more be confounded, until the end come when the earth shall pass away. And there shall be a new heaven and a new earth; and they shall be like unto the old save the old have passed away, and all things have become new.
>
> And then cometh the New Jerusalem; and blessed are they who dwell therein, for it is they whose garments are white through the blood of the Lamb; and *they are they who are numbered among the remnant of the seed of Joseph*, who were of the house of Israel. (Ether 13:6-10)

There is another important aspect of Zion, or The New Jerusalem, that Isaiah described:

> And I [**the Lord**] will restore thy judges as at the first, and thy counsellors as at the beginning: afterward thou shalt be called, The city of righteousness, the

faithful city. *Zion shall be redeemed with judgment*, and her converts with righteousness. (Isaiah 1:26-27)

The entire purpose for Zion, or the New Jerusalem will be to restore "the law" (Isaiah 2:3) as at first, with righteous judges and counselors. This will restore freedom. An important principle of God's *Art of War* is Principle #5: *The inward vessel shall be cleansed first... even the great head of our government.* (Alma 60:23-24) Once the government is cleansed, *righteous* armies will be directed solely in defense of life, liberty and property, as Moroni so boldly declared should be the case (in Alma 46:12-13; see also Alma 59:13, Helaman 1:7-8, and the entire chapter of Alma 60).

For more detail on the New Jerusalem, please read the chapter entitled "Kingdom of God", wherein Brigham Young expounds on how the law will be administered in great detail.

President John Taylor, who succeeded Brigham Young, while speaking on August 31, 1879 in Logan Utah, gave additional insight into this futuristic godly city, and its primary mission to protect civil law. Said he:

"...The day is not far distant when this nation will be shaken from centre to circumference. And now, you may write it down, any of you, and I will prophesy it in the name of God. And then will be fulfilled that prediction to be found in one of the revelations given through the Prophet Joseph Smith. Those who will not take up their sword to fight against their neighbor [**offensive war**] must needs flee to Zion for safety [**defensive war**]. (D&C 45:68) And they will come, saying, we do not know anything of the principles of your religion, but we perceive that you are an honest community; you administer justice and righteousness, and we want to live with you and receive the protection of your laws, but as for your religion we will talk about that some other time. Will we protect such people? Yes, all honorable men. When the people shall have torn to shreds the Constitution of the United States the Elders of Israel will be found holding it up to the nations of the earth and proclaiming liberty and equal rights to all men, and extending the hand of fellowship to the oppressed of all nations." (John Taylor, Journal of Discourses, 21:8)

The remainder of Jesus' prophecy to the Ancient Americans in 3 Nephi 16 can be found in 3 Nephi Chapters 20 & 21, in which Jesus picks up right where he left off.

From 3rd Nephi 20:

> ...now I finish the commandment which the Father hath commanded me concerning this people, who are a remnant of the house of Israel. Ye remember that I spake unto you, and said that when the words of Isaiah should be fulfilled... then is the fulfilling of the covenant which the Father hath made unto his people, O house of Israel... And the Father hath commanded me that I should give unto you this land, for your inheritance.
>
> And I say unto you, that if the Gentiles do not repent after the blessing which they shall receive [**from our Founding Fathers, being given this land of America as a *free* land, and now forsaking this freedom**], after they

have scattered my people— Then shall ye, who are a remnant of the house of Jacob [**American Indians**], go forth among them; and ye shall be in the midst of them who shall be many; and ye shall be among them as a lion among the beasts of the forest, and as a young lion among the flocks of sheep, who, if he goeth through both treadeth down and teareth in pieces, and none can deliver. Thy hand shall be lifted up upon thine adversaries, and all thine enemies shall be cut off.

And I will gather my people together as a man gathereth his sheaves into the floor. For I will make my people with whom the Father hath covenanted, yea, I will make thy horn iron, and I will make thy hoofs brass. And thou shalt beat in pieces many people… And it shall come to pass, saith the Father, that the sword of my justice shall hang over them [**Gentiles**] at that day; and except they repent it shall fall upon them, saith the Father, yea, even upon all the nations of the Gentiles. And it shall come to pass that I will establish my people, O house of Israel [**American Indians & Jews**].

And behold, this people [**children of whom He is speaking to, the American Indians**] will I establish in this land, unto the fulfilling of the covenant which I made with your father Jacob; and it shall be a New Jerusalem [**Zion at Independence, Missouri**]. And the powers of heaven shall be in the midst of this people [**American Indians**]; yea, even I will be in the midst of you...

And behold, ye [**of whom He is speaking to, the American Indians**] are the children of the prophets; and ye are of the house of Israel; and ye are of the covenant which the Father made with your fathers, saying unto Abraham: And in thy seed shall all the kindreds of the earth be blessed [**by restoring freedom and freedom principles**]...

From 3rd Nephi 21:

And verily I say unto you, I give unto you a sign, that ye may know the time when these things shall be about to take place—that I shall gather in, from their long dispersion my people [**not since the Book of Mormon times have the Indians had the fullness of the gospel**], O house of Israel, and shall establish again among them my Zion;

And behold, this is the thing which I will give unto you for a sign—... *For it is wisdom in the Father that they should be established in this land, and be set up as a free people by the power of the Father* [**The Founding Fathers work**], *that these things might come forth from them unto a remnant of your seed* [**American Indians**], that the covenant of the Father may be fulfilled which he hath covenanted with his people, O house of Israel;

Therefore, when *these works* [**being "set up as a free people"**]... shall come forth from the Gentiles, unto your seed which shall dwindle in unbelief because of iniquity;... *that thy seed shall begin to know these things* [**the freedom principles, taught by righteous gentiles**]—it shall be a sign unto them, that they may know that the work of the Father hath already commenced unto the fulfilling of the covenant which he hath made unto the people who are of the house of Israel...

And when that day shall come, it shall come to pass that kings shall shut their mouths; for that which had not been told them shall they see; and that which they had not heard shall they consider [**that the Latter-day Lamanites are no longer the dark, filthy, loathsome idlers shown to Nephi in 1 Nephi 12:23, but a Christ-believing, righteous, and undefeatable group of warriors for God, fulfilling their divine, though unbelievable to some, destiny**].

And my people who are a remnant of Jacob [**American Indians**] shall be among the Gentiles [**wicked Gentiles who want to war against Freedom principles, and again subjugate the people**], yea, in the midst of them as a lion among the beasts of the forest, as a young lion among the flocks of sheep, who, if he go through both treadeth down and teareth in pieces, and none can deliver. Their hand shall be lifted up upon their adversaries, and all their enemies shall be cut off...

And they [**the righteous Gentiles**] shall assist my people, the remnant of Jacob [**American Indians**], and also as many of the house of Israel as shall come, that they may build a city, which shall be called the New Jerusalem [**Independence, Missouri, or Zion**]. And then shall they [**the righteous Gentiles**] assist my people [**American Indians**] that they may be gathered in, who are scattered upon all the face of the land, in unto the New Jerusalem. And then shall the power of heaven come down among them; and I also will be in the midst.

Yea, and then shall the work commence, with the Father among all nations in preparing the way whereby his people may be gathered home to the land of their inheritance.

Principle 7 in God's *Art of War*: *Love your Enemies, Pray for your Enemies, Do not Delight in Killing*

> Ye have heard that it hath been said, Thou shalt love thy neighbour, and hate thine enemy. But I say unto you, Love your enemies, bless them that curse you, do good to them that hate you, and pray for them which despitefully use you, and persecute you; That ye may be the children of your Father which is in heaven: for he maketh his sun to rise on the evil and on the good, and sendeth rain on the just and on the unjust.
>
> For if ye love them which love you, what reward have ye? (Matthew 5:43-46)

Despite this teaching of our Savior, numerous evidences are that Americans don't live by a "love your neighbor" philosophy. Barack Obama's leadership, for example, is that Matthew 5:43-46 is "so radical that it's doubtful that our own defense department could survive its application." Then mockingly taunts, "You folks haven't been reading your Bibles, have you..?" (*Call to Renewal Confere*nce, June 28, 2006) And he's in good company. Most politicians agree, from the Bills they pass and illegal actions they allow, in a position of *hate* your enemy, *war with* your enemy, and do it *on their soil*.

In a 2012 presidential debate, the audience loudly booed when Ron Paul suggested we, as Americans, follow the golden rule when it comes to foreign policy. (*"Fox/Twitter Debate: Republicans Loudly "Boo" the Golden Rule"*, The New American, January 17th, 2012) The Golden Rule is a key part of Christianity and all other major world religions. In the Bible, Jesus Christ himself commands the Golden Rule (Matthew 7:12, Luke 6:31):

> Therefore all things whatsoever ye would that men should do to you, do ye even so to them: for this is the law and the prophets. (Matthew 7:12)

President Spencer W. Kimball sums up the nature of our country's rancid soul by saying, in 1976:

> "*We are a warlike people*, easily distracted from our assignment of preparing for the coming of the Lord. When enemies rise up, we commit vast resources to the fabrication of gods of stone and steel—ships, planes, missiles, fortifications—and depend on them for

protection and deliverance. When threatened, we become anti-enemy instead of pro-kingdom of God; we train a man in the *Art of War* and call him a patriot, thus, in the manner of Satan's counterfeit of true patriotism, perverting the Savior's teaching: *Love your enemies, bless them that curse you, do good to them that hate you, and pray for them which despitefully use you, and persecute you; That ye may be the children of your Father which is in heaven."* (*The False Gods We Worship*, Conference Report, 1976)

Mormon was killed in battle to the Lamanites, as recorded by his son, Moroni (Mormon 8:5). This is after witnessing a lifetime of brutality, carnage, rape, and human sacrifice by a people who caused his people, the Nephites, to become extinct. This caused Mormon great lamenting as he stood atop hill Cumorah looking over a half-million dead bodies, including all of his remaining brethren. The irony in this scene is that at the same time he was sorrowful at the final reality of his people's fate, Mormon felt deep love, and even *respect*, for a brutal and bloodthirsty foe. This respect came because Mormon knew their destiny, and the covenant God would later fulfill among the Latter-day Lamanites.

As his final words, before handing the sacred plates over to his son, Moroni, he desired a chance to say a few words to his brethren for whom, even in their wickedness, captivated his heart:

> And now, behold, I would speak somewhat unto the remnant of this people who are spared, if it so be that God may give unto them my words, that they may know of the things of their fathers; yea, I speak unto you, ye remnant of the house of Israel; and these are the words which I speak: Know ye that ye are of the house of Israel. Know ye that ye must come unto repentance, or ye cannot be saved. Know ye that ye must lay down your weapons of war, and delight no more in the shedding of blood, and take them not again, save it be that God shall command you.
>
> Know ye that ye must come to the knowledge of your fathers, and repent of all your sins and iniquities, and believe in Jesus Christ, that he is the

Son of God, and that he was slain by the Jews, and by the power of the Father he hath risen again, whereby he hath gained the victory over the grave; and also in him is the sting of death swallowed up. And he bringeth to pass the resurrection of the dead, whereby man must be raised to stand before his judgment-seat.

And he hath brought to pass the redemption of the world, whereby he that is found guiltless before him at the judgment day hath it given unto him to dwell in the presence of God in his kingdom, to sing ceaseless praises with the choirs above, unto the Father, and unto the Son, and unto the Holy Ghost, which are one God, in a state of happiness which hath no end.

Therefore repent, and be baptized in the name of Jesus, and lay hold upon the gospel of Christ, which shall be set before you, not only in this record but also in the record which shall come unto the Gentiles from the Jews, which record shall come from the Gentiles unto you.

For behold, this is written for the intent that ye may believe that; and if ye believe that ye will believe this also; and if ye believe this ye will know concerning your fathers, and also the marvelous works which were wrought by the power of God among them.

And ye will also know that ye are a remnant of the seed of Jacob; therefore ye are numbered among the people of the first covenant; and if it so be that ye believe in Christ, and are baptized, first with water, then with fire and with the Holy Ghost, following the example of our Savior, according to that which he hath commanded us, it shall be well with you in the day of judgment. Amen. (Mormon 7)

Mormon's example is one of love towards his enemies.

Jesus Christ' Foreordination of the Indian People, as recorded in 3 Nephi 21

In Isaiah, 52:15 it states:

> So shall he sprinkle many nations; the kings shall shut their mouths at him: for that which had not been told them shall they see; and that which they had not heard shall they consider.

A common principle in discerning scriptural text is that some of what is written is purposefully designed to be concealed from the masses, and available only to those who learn to encapsulate and develop the spirit of prophesy and revelation. For Nephi says:

> For behold, Isaiah spake many things which were hard for many of my people to understand; for they know not concerning the manner of prophesying among the Jews... Wherefore, hearken,

> O my people, which are of the house of Israel, and give ear unto my words; *for because the words of Isaiah are not plain unto you, nevertheless they are plain unto all those that are filled with the spirit of prophecy.* (2 Nephi 25:4)

In 3 Nephi 21 Jesus clarifies some of what Isaiah says, including the previous scripture (of Isaiah 52:15).

To begin with, He states:

> And verily I say unto you, I give unto you a **sign**, that ye may know the **time** when **these things** shall be about to take place… (3rd Nephi 21:1)

Seldom does the Lord give signs. But here Jesus clearly allows us one—specifically the *time* in which these things will take place. What things?

> …that I shall gather in, from their long dispersion, my people, O house of Israel [**the Indian people**], and shall establish again among them my Zion.

This will be a time when the world will begin to be established, or governed, according to righteousness in government, for "out of Zion shall go forth the law." (Isaiah 2:3)

Furthermore:

> ...for verily I say unto you that when these things which I declare unto you... shall be made known unto the Gentiles that they may know concerning this people who are a remnant of the house of Jacob, and concerning this my people who shall be scattered by them... (3rd Nephi 21:2)

The Gentiles are those who are NOT of the blood of Israel—NON-Indians and NON-Jews. The Gentiles make up the majority of the population of America.

Jesus states that there will come a time when the Gentiles will know concerning the covenants made unto the Indian people. Jesus also states that these Indians will be "scattered" by the Gentiles—which has certainly happened.

Continuing:

> Verily, verily, I say unto you, when these things shall be made known unto them *of* the Father, and shall come forth *of* the Father, from them unto you... (3rd Nephi 21:3)

Evidently, the Indian people, who are the posterity of those to whom Jesus is speaking to, will NOT know of the Lord's covenant to "this people who are a remnant of the House of Jacob." They will learn of this covenant *from the Gentiles*, for this great knowledge of their destiny will come, "of the Father, from them [Gentiles] unto you." Hence this knowledge is FROM God TO the Gentiles, then FROM the Gentiles TO the Indian people.

Jesus even goes so far as to say that when the Indian people do received this knowledge, it will be a great light unto them since prior to this time they will have "dwindle[d] in unbelief because of iniquity." (3rd Nephi 21:5)

But what results will knowing the details of the covenant bring?

Continuing:

> For it is wisdom in the Father that *they* **[the covenants or knowledge of the destiny of the Indian people]** should be established in this land, and be *set up as a free people* by the power of the Father, that these things might come forth from them [**Gentiles**] unto a remnant of your seed, that the

> covenant of the Father may be fulfilled which he hath covenanted with his people, O house of Israel; (3rd Nephi 21:4)

Gentiles, or our Founding Fathers, are who established liberty to this land in the late 18th century. This establishment of freedom principles, with power to perpetuate a society into the eternities, will be preserved by the Indian people. THIS is the central theme of the covenant—the restoration of freedom to this land through adherence and worship of Jesus Christ.

In 2012 America, the Indian people at large do NOT know that this is their calling and destiny, but IT WILL HAPPEN. Jesus makes this clear. This author doesn't use the word "destiny" loosely because many things in the scriptures are IF-THEN statements, meaning an involvement of choice. But in this prophecy, Jesus Christ says THIS WILL HAPPEN.

To finish:

> And when these things come to pass that thy seed shall begin to know these things—it shall be a sign unto them, that they may know that the work of the Father hath already commenced

> unto the fulfilling of the covenant which he hath made unto the people who are of the house of Israel. (3rd Nephi 21:7)

In other words, when the Indian people shall begin to embrace their destiny—first by learning the principles of freedom's preservation as part of the "fulness" of the gospel", and then defending liberty's cause with the sword, then the "work of the Father [**will have**] already commenced" in fulfilling of the Lord's covenant to the House of Israel.

> And my people who are a remnant of Jacob [**American Indians**] shall be among the Gentiles, yea, in the midst of them as a lion among the beasts of the forest, as a young lion among the flocks of sheep, who, if he go through both treadeth down and teareth in pieces, and none can deliver. Their hand shall be lifted up upon their adversaries, and all their enemies shall be cut off. (3rd Nephi 21:12-13, also quoted in Isaiah 5:29, and Micah 5:8 in the Old Testament)

THIS is the power that the Indian people will have. Today the Indian people have been scattered across the American continent. They are generally known as an indolent people, full of idleness and idolatry—alcohol drinkers, operators of casinos, and voters of those who will redistribute other's wealth to them. According to data collected from the Center for Disease Control website, the top 30 Indian Counties in America collectively rank among the very top of 3,100+ counties in rate of "Inactivity," "Obesity," and "Diabetes."

However, when the Indian people begin to understand their true calling and destiny—to preserve freedom *in the strength of the Lord* using the 24 war-principles pulled from the pages of the Book of Mormon (and contained in this book), they will become the most powerful people on Earth—all this according to Jesus Christ Himself.

> And when that day shall come, it shall come to pass that kings shall shut their mouths; for that which had not been told them shall they see; and that which they had not heard shall they consider. (3rd Nephi 21:8)

That all this would occur, and that the Indian people would be God's primary instrument in fulfilling such a destiny as this, by the annihilation of anyone they oppose, is something virtually no one, including our world's nations of Kings, would ever consider as plausible.

In verse 10 Jesus goes into still more detail about how this epic transition of the Indian nations will occur. Here Jesus refers to "my servant," and says in the next verse:

> Therefore it shall come to pass that whosoever will not believe in my words, who am Jesus Christ, which the Father **shall cause *him* to bring forth**... shall be cut off from among my people who are of the covenant. (3rd Nephi 21:11)

Who is this person, this *servant*, whom Jesus is referring to? Would it not be the person for whom the Lord used to spring this knowledge into existence in the latter days? Would it not be the primary person whom the Lord used to bring about the conditions that would convince and convert the Indians to come unto Christ? Would it not be the person who brought the sacred volume of The Book of Mormon out of the ground, for it to go forth, convincing the Indian people of both their past and future—with the knowledge that they are of the House of Israel, and that their destiny is that of understanding and completely internalizing this holy record, from which these revelations come?

Would not this servant be Joseph Smith, and thus would not the name of Joseph Smith be highly esteemed among the Indian people?

The Indian people are a remnant of the seed of Jacob through Joseph, his son, and…:

> Joseph truly said: Thus saith the Lord unto me: A choice seer [**Joseph Smith**] will I raise up out of the fruit of thy loins; and he ***shall be esteemed highly*** among the fruit of thy loins. And unto him will I give commandment that he shall do a work for the fruit of thy loins, his brethren [**the Indian people**], which shall be of great worth unto them, even to the bringing of them to the knowledge of the covenants which I have made with thy fathers. (2nd Nephi 3:7)
>
> And his name shall be called after me; and it shall be after the name of his father [**Joseph Smith Sr.**]. And he shall be like unto me; for the thing, which the Lord shall bring forth by his hand,

> by the power of the Lord shall bring my people unto salvation.
>
> Yea, thus prophesied Joseph [**Jacob's son**]: I am sure of this thing, even as I am sure of the promise of Moses; for the Lord hath said unto me, I will preserve thy seed forever. (2 Nephi 3:15-16)

Again, these are facts, according to prophecy. The invitation to the Indian people across the American continent is to rise up and begin to believe in the Book of Mormon, in Joseph Smith, and in your divine destiny to restore again and perpetuate freedom through being the warriors that you are—godly warriors who believe in Jesus Christ and in His power to make you invincible as you go forth *in the strength of the Lord*.

When this happens, the Indian people are going to lead the charge to Zion, or the New Jerusalem, from which God's Law of Freedom and Independence will go forth. The righteous Gentile's role will be only to assist the Indians in that effort, and eventually to be themselves numbered with the Indians, adopted into the House of Israel.

For Jesus states:

> And they [**the Gentiles**] shall assist my people, the remnant of Jacob, and also as many of the house of Israel as shall come, that they may build a city, which shall be called the New Jerusalem [**in Independence, Missouri**]. And then shall they assist my people that they may be gathered in, who are scattered upon all the face of the land, in unto the New Jerusalem.
>
> Yea, and then shall the work commence, with the Father among all nations in preparing the way whereby his people may be gathered home to the land of their inheritance. (3rd Nephi 23-24, 28)

As well, From Elder Orson Pratt:

> What says the Book of Mormon in relation to the building up of the New Jerusalem on this continent one of the most splendid cities that ever was or ever will be built on this land? Does not that book say that the Lamanites are to be the principal operators in that important work, and that those who embrace the Gospel from among the

> Gentiles are to have the privilege of assisting the Lamanites to build up the city called the New Jerusalem? This remnant of Joseph, who are now degraded, will then be filled with the wisdom of God; and by that wisdom they will build that city; by the aid of the Priesthood already given, and by the aid of Prophets that God will raise up in their midst, they will beautify and ornament its dwellings; and we have the privilege of being numbered with them, instead of their being numbered with us. It is a great privilege indeed (and we are indebted to their fathers for it,) that we enjoy of being associated with them in the accomplishment of so great a work. (JD 9:178)

Since the Indian people, or latter-day Lamanites, are to lead this charge, this author invite those with the spirit of leadership among you to "lead the charge" of your people. At the beginning of a change, the Lord always asks for "leaders of leaders." Be that leader, and wear the honor of a Lamanite Patriot!

> In the beginning of a change the patriot is a scarce man—brave, and hated and

scorned. When his cause succeeds [however], the timid join him, for then it costs nothing to be a patriot. —Mark Twain, 1904

Sun Tzu's The Art of War

I. Laying Plans

1. Sun Tzu said: The *Art of War* is of vital importance to the State.

2. It is a matter of life and death, a road either to safety or to ruin. Hence it is a subject of inquiry which can on no account be neglected.

3. The *Art of War*, then, is governed by five constant factors, to be taken into account in one's deliberations, when seeking to determine the conditions obtaining in the field.

4. These are: (1) The Moral Law; (2) Heaven; (3) Earth; (4) The Commander; (5) Method and discipline.

5, 6. The MORAL LAW causes the people to be in complete accord with their ruler, so that they will follow him regardless of their lives, undismayed by any danger.

7. HEAVEN signifies night and day, cold and heat, times and seasons.

8. EARTH comprises distances, great and small; danger and security; open ground and narrow passes; the chances of life and death.

9. The COMMANDER stands for the virtues of wisdom, sincerely, benevolence, courage and strictness.

10. By METHOD AND DISCIPLINE are to be understood the marshaling of the army in its proper subdivisions, the graduations of rank among the officers, the maintenance of roads by which supplies may reach the army, and the control of military expenditure.

11. These five heads should be familiar to every general: he who knows them will be victorious; he who knows them not will fail.

12. Therefore, in your deliberations, when seeking to determine the military conditions, let them be made the basis of a comparison, in this wise:

13. (1) Which of the two sovereigns is imbued with the Moral law?

    (2) Which of the two generals has most ability?

    (3) With whom lie the advantages derived from Heaven and Earth?

    (4) On which side is discipline most rigorously enforced?

    (5) Which army is stronger?

    (6) On which side are officers and men more highly trained?

    (7) In which army is there the greater constancy both in reward and punishment?

14. By means of these seven considerations I can forecast victory or defeat.

15. The general that hearkens to my counsel and acts upon it, will conquer: let such a one be retained in command! The general that hearkens not to my counsel nor acts upon it, will suffer defeat: let such a one be dismissed!

16. While heading the profit of my counsel, avail yourself also of any helpful circumstances over and beyond the ordinary rules.

17. According as circumstances are favorable, one should modify one's plans.

> Sun Tzu cautions us here not to pin our faith to abstract principles; for, as Chang Yu puts it, "while the main laws of strategy can be stated clearly enough for the benefit of all and sundry, you must be guided by the actions of the enemy in attempting to secure a favorable position in actual warfare." On the eve of the battle of Waterloo, Lord Uxbridge, commanding the cavalry, went to the Duke of Wellington in order to learn what his plans and calculations were for the morrow, because, as he explained, he might suddenly find himself Commander-in-chief and would be unable to frame new plans in a critical moment. The Duke listened quietly and then said: "Who will attack the first tomorrow, I or Bonaparte?" "Bonaparte," replied Lord Uxbridge. "Well," continued the Duke, "Bonaparte has not given me any idea of his projects; and as my plans will

depend upon his, how can you expect me to tell you what mine are?" ("Words on Wellington," by Sir. W. Fraser)

18. All warfare is based on deception.

19. Hence, when able to attack, we must seem unable; when using our forces, we must seem inactive; when we are near, we must make the enemy believe we are far away; when far away, we must make him believe we are near.

20. Hold out baits to entice the enemy. Feign disorder, and crush him.

21. If he is secure at all points, be prepared for him. If he is in superior strength, evade him.

22. If your opponent is of choleric temper, seek to irritate him. Pretend to be weak, that he may grow arrogant.

23. If he is taking his ease, give him no rest. If his forces are united, separate them.

24. Attack him where he is unprepared, appear where you are not expected.

25. These military devices, leading to victory, must not be divulged beforehand.

26. Now the general who wins a battle makes many calculations in his temple ere the battle is fought. The general who loses a battle makes but few calculations beforehand. Thus do many calculations lead to victory, and few calculations to defeat: how much more no calculation at all! It is by attention to this point that I can foresee who is likely to win or lose.

II. Waging War

1. Sun Tzu said: In the operations of war, where there are in the field a thousand swift chariots, as many heavy chariots, and a hundred thousand mail-clad soldiers, with provisions enough to carry them a thousand LI, the expenditure at home and at the front, including entertainment of guests, small items such as glue and paint, and sums spent on chariots and armor, will reach the total of a thousand ounces of

silver per day. Such is the cost of raising an army of 100,000 men.

2. When you engage in actual fighting, if victory is long in coming, then men's weapons will grow dull and their ardor will be damped. If you lay siege to a town, you will exhaust your strength.

3. Again, if the campaign is protracted, the resources of the State will not be equal to the strain.

4. Now, when your weapons are dulled, your ardor damped, your strength exhausted and your treasure spent, other chieftains will spring up to take advantage of your extremity. Then no man, however wise, will be able to avert the consequences that must ensue.

5. Thus, though we have heard of stupid haste in war, cleverness has never been seen associated with long delays.

6. There is no instance of a country having benefited from prolonged warfare.

7. It is only one who is thoroughly acquainted with the evils of war that can thoroughly

understand the profitable way of carrying it on.

8. The skillful soldier does not raise a second levy, neither are his supply-wagons loaded more than twice.

9. Bring war material with you from home, but forage on the enemy. Thus the army will have food enough for its needs.

10. Poverty of the State exchequer causes an army to be maintained by contributions from a distance. Contributing to maintain an army at a distance causes the people to be impoverished.

11. On the other hand, the proximity of an army causes prices to go up; and high prices cause the people's substance to be drained away.

12. When their substance is drained away, the peasantry will be afflicted by heavy exactions.

13, 14. With this loss of substance and exhaustion of strength, the homes of the people will be stripped bare, and three-tenths of their income will be dissipated;

while government expenses for broken chariots, worn-out horses, breast-plates and helmets, bows and arrows, spears and shields, protective mantles, draught-oxen and heavy wagons, will amount to four-tenths of its total revenue.

15. Hence a wise general makes a point of foraging on the enemy. One cartload of the enemy's provisions is equivalent to twenty of one's own, and likewise a single PICUL (133 pounds) of his provender is equivalent to twenty from one's own store.

16. Now in order to kill the enemy, our men must be roused to anger; that there may be advantage from defeating the enemy, they must have their rewards.

17. Therefore in chariot fighting, when ten or more chariots have been taken, those should be rewarded who took the first. Our own flags should be substituted for those of the enemy, and the chariots mingled and used in conjunction with ours. The captured soldiers should be kindly treated and kept.

18. This is called, using the conquered foe to augment one's own strength.

19. In war, then, let your great object be victory, not lengthy campaigns.

20. Thus it may be known that the leader of armies is the arbiter of the people's fate, the man on whom it depends whether the nation shall be in peace or in peril.

III. Attack by Strategem

1. Sun Tzu said: In the practical *Art of War*, the best thing of all is to take the enemy's country whole and intact; to shatter and destroy it is not so good. So, too, it is better to recapture an army entire than to destroy it, to capture a regiment, a detachment or a company entire than to destroy them.

2. Hence to fight and conquer in all your battles is not supreme excellence; supreme excellence consists in breaking the enemy's resistance without fighting.

   Another version of this principle is: *For to win one hundred victories in one hundred battles is not the acme of skill. To subdue the enemy without fighting is the acme of skill.*

3. Thus the highest form of generalship is to balk (an active policy of counter-attack) the enemy's plans; the next best is to prevent the junction of the enemy's forces; the next in order is to attack the enemy's army in the field; and the worst policy of all is to besiege walled cities.

4. The rule is, not to besiege walled cities if it can possibly be avoided. The preparation of mantlets, movable shelters, and various implements of war, will take up three whole months; and the piling up of mounds over against the walls will take three months more.

5. The general, unable to control his irritation, will launch his men to the assault like swarming ants, with the result that one-third of his men are slain, while the town still remains untaken. Such are the disastrous effects of a siege.

6. Therefore the skillful leader subdues the enemy's troops without any fighting; he

captures their cities without laying siege to them; he overthrows their kingdom without lengthy operations in the field.

7. With his forces intact he will dispute the mastery of the Empire, and thus, without losing a man, his triumph will be complete. This is the method of attacking by stratagem.

8. It is the rule in war, if our forces are ten to the enemy's one, to surround him; if five to one, to attack him; if twice as numerous, to divide our army into two.

9. If equally matched, we can offer battle; if slightly inferior in numbers, we can avoid the enemy; if quite unequal in every way, we can flee from him.

10. Hence, though an obstinate fight may be made by a small force, in the end it must be captured by the larger force.

11. Now the general is the bulwark of the State; if the bulwark is complete at all points; the State will be strong; if the bulwark is defective, the State will be weak.

12. There are three ways in which a ruler can bring misfortune upon his army:

13. (1) By commanding the army to advance or to retreat, being ignorant of the fact that it cannot obey. This is called hobbling the army.

14. (2) By attempting to govern an army in the same way as he administers a kingdom, being ignorant of the conditions which obtain in an army. This causes restlessness in the soldier's minds.

15. (3) By employing the officers of his army without discrimination, through ignorance of the military principle of adaptation to circumstances. This shakes the confidence of the soldiers.

16. But when the army is restless and distrustful, trouble is sure to come from the other feudal princes. This is simply bringing anarchy into the army, and flinging victory away.

17. Thus we may know that there are five essentials for victory: (1) He will win who knows when to fight and when not to fight. (2) He will win who knows how to handle

both superior and inferior forces. (3) He will win whose army is animated by the same spirit throughout all its ranks. (4) He will win who, prepared himself, waits to take the enemy unprepared. (5) He will win who has military capacity and is not interfered with by the sovereign.

18. Hence the saying: If you know the enemy and know yourself, you need not fear the result of a hundred battles. If you know yourself but not the enemy, for every victory gained you will also suffer a defeat. If you know neither the enemy nor yourself, you will succumb in every battle.

IV. Tactical Dispositions

1. Sun Tzu said: The good fighters of old first put themselves beyond the possibility of defeat, and then waited for an opportunity of defeating the enemy.

2. To secure ourselves against defeat lies in our own hands, but the opportunity of defeating the enemy is provided by the enemy himself.

3. Thus the good fighter is able to secure himself against defeat, but cannot make certain of defeating the enemy.

4. Hence the saying: One may KNOW how to conquer without being able to DO it.

5. Security against defeat implies defensive tactics; ability to defeat the enemy means taking the offensive.

6. Standing on the defensive indicates insufficient strength; attacking, a superabundance of strength.

7. The general who is skilled in defense hides in the most secret recesses of the earth; he who is skilled in attack flashes forth from the topmost heights of heaven. Thus on the one hand we have ability to protect ourselves; on the other, a victory that is complete.

8. To see victory only when it is within the ken of the common herd is not the acme of excellence.

9. Neither is it the acme of excellence if you fight and conquer and the whole Empire says, "Well done!"

10. To lift an autumn hair is no sign of great strength; to see the sun and moon is no sign of sharp sight; to hear the noise of thunder is no sign of a quick ear.

11. What the ancients called a clever fighter is one who not only wins, but excels in winning with ease.

12. Hence his victories bring him neither reputation for wisdom nor credit for courage.

13. He wins his battles by making no mistakes. Making no mistakes is what establishes the certainty of victory, for it means conquering an enemy that is already defeated.

14. Hence the skillful fighter puts himself into a position which makes defeat impossible, and does not miss the moment for defeating the enemy.

15. Thus it is that in war the victorious strategist only seeks battle after the victory has been won, whereas he who is destined to defeat first fights and afterwards looks for victory.

16. The consummate leader cultivates the moral law, and strictly adheres to method and discipline; thus it is in his power to control success.

17. In respect of military method, we have, firstly, Measurement; secondly, Estimation of quantity; thirdly, Calculation; fourthly, Balancing of chances; fifthly, Victory.

18. Measurement owes its existence to Earth; Estimation of quantity to Measurement; Calculation to Estimation of quantity;

Balancing of chances to Calculation; and Victory to Balancing of chances.

19. A victorious army opposed to a routed one, is as a pound's weight placed in the scale against a single grain.

20. The onrush of a conquering force is like the bursting of pent-up waters into a chasm a thousand fathoms deep.

V. Energy

1. Sun Tzu said: The control of a large force is the same principle as the control of a few men: it is merely a question of dividing up their numbers.

2. Fighting with a large army under your command is nowise different from fighting with a small one: it is merely a question of instituting signs and signals.

3. To ensure that your whole host may withstand the brunt of the enemy's attack and remain unshaken - this is effected by maneuvers direct and indirect.

4. That the impact of your army may be like a grindstone dashed against an egg - this is effected by the science of weak points and strong.

5. In all fighting, the direct method may be used for joining battle, but indirect methods will be needed in order to secure victory.

6. Indirect tactics, efficiently applied, are inexhaustible as Heaven and Earth, unending as the flow of rivers and streams; like the sun and moon, they end but to begin anew; like the four seasons, they pass away to return once more.

7. There are not more than five musical notes, yet the combinations of these five give rise to more melodies than can ever be heard.

8. There are not more than five primary colors (blue, yellow, red, white, and black), yet in combination they produce more hues than can ever been seen.

9. There are not more than five cardinal tastes (sour, acrid, salt, sweet, bitter), yet combinations of them yield more flavors than can ever be tasted.

10. In battle, there are not more than two methods of attack - the direct and the indirect; yet these two in combination give rise to an endless series of maneuvers.

11. The direct and the indirect lead on to each other in turn. It is like moving in a circle - you never come to an end. Who can exhaust the possibilities of their combination?

12. The onset of troops is like the rush of a torrent which will even roll stones along in its course.

13. The quality of decision is like the well-timed swoop of a falcon which enables it to strike and destroy its victim.

14. Therefore the good fighter will be terrible in his onset, and prompt in his decision.

15. Energy may be likened to the bending of a crossbow; decision, to the releasing of a trigger.

16. Amid the turmoil and tumult of battle, there may be seeming disorder and yet no real disorder at all; amid confusion and

chaos, your array may be without head or tail, yet it will be proof against defeat.

17. Simulated disorder postulates perfect discipline, simulated fear postulates courage; simulated weakness postulates strength.

18. Hiding order beneath the cloak of disorder is simply a question of subdivision; concealing courage under a show of timidity presupposes a fund of latent energy; masking strength with weakness is to be effected by tactical dispositions.

19. Thus one who is skillful at keeping the enemy on the move maintains deceitful appearances, according to which the enemy will act. He sacrifices something, that the enemy may snatch at it.

20. By holding out baits, he keeps him on the march; then with a body of picked men he lies in wait for him.

21. The clever combatant looks to the effect of combined energy, and does not require too much from individuals. Hence his ability to pick out the right men and utilize combined energy.

22. When he utilizes combined energy, his fighting men become as it were like unto rolling logs or stones. For it is the nature of a log or stone to remain motionless on level ground, and to move when on a slope; if four-cornered, to come to a standstill, but if round-shaped, to go rolling down.

23. Thus the energy developed by good fighting men is as the momentum of a round stone rolled down a mountain thousands of feet in height. So much on the subject of energy.

VI. Weak Points and Strong

1. Sun Tzu said: Whoever is first in the field and awaits the coming of the enemy, will be fresh for the fight; whoever is second in the field and has to hasten to battle will arrive exhausted.

2. Therefore the clever combatant imposes his will on the enemy, but does not allow the enemy's will to be imposed on him.

3. By holding out advantages to him, he can cause the enemy to approach of his own accord; or, by inflicting damage, he can make it impossible for the enemy to draw near.

4. If the enemy is taking his ease, he can harass him; if well supplied with food, he can starve him out; if quietly encamped, he can force him to move.

5. Appear at points which the enemy must hasten to defend; march swiftly to places where you are not expected.

6. An army may march great distances without distress, if it marches through country where the enemy is not.

7. You can be sure of succeeding in your attacks if you only attack places which are undefended. You can ensure the safety of your defense if you only hold positions that cannot be attacked.

8. Hence that general is skillful in attack whose opponent does not know what to defend; and he is skillful in defense whose opponent does not know what to attack.

9. O divine art of subtlety and secrecy! Through you we learn to be invisible, through you inaudible; and hence we can hold the enemy's fate in our hands.

10. You may advance and be absolutely irresistible, if you make for the enemy's weak points; you may retire and be safe from pursuit if your movements are more rapid than those of the enemy.

11. If we wish to fight, the enemy can be forced to an engagement even though he be sheltered behind a high rampart and a deep ditch. All we need do is attack some other place that he will be obliged to relieve.

12. If we do not wish to fight, we can prevent the enemy from engaging us even though the lines of our encampment be merely traced out on the ground. All we need do is to throw something odd and unaccountable in his way.

13. By discovering the enemy's dispositions and remaining invisible ourselves, we can keep our forces concentrated, while the enemy's must be divided.

14. We can form a single united body, while the enemy must split up into fractions. Hence there will be a whole pitted against separate parts of a whole, which means that we shall be many to the enemy's few.

15. And if we are able thus to attack an inferior force with a superior one, our opponents will be in dire straits.

16. The spot where we intend to fight must not be made known; for then the enemy will have to prepare against a possible attack at several different points; and his forces being thus distributed in many directions, the numbers we shall have to face at any given point will be proportionately few.

17. For should the enemy strengthen his van, he will weaken his rear; should he strengthen his rear, he will weaken his van; should he strengthen his left, he will weaken his right; should he strengthen his right, he will weaken his left. If he sends reinforcements everywhere, he will everywhere be weak.

18. Numerical weakness comes from having to prepare against possible attacks; numerical

strength, from compelling our adversary to make these preparations against us.

19. Knowing the place and the time of the coming battle, we may concentrate from the greatest distances in order to fight.

20. But if neither time nor place be known, then the left wing will be impotent to succor the right, the right equally impotent to succor the left, the van unable to relieve the rear, or the rear to support the van. How much more so if the furthest portions of the army are anything under a hundred LI (a third of a mile) apart, and even the nearest are separated by several LI!

21. Though according to my estimate the soldiers of Yueh exceed our own in number, that shall advantage them nothing in the matter of victory. I say then that victory can be achieved.

22. Though the enemy be stronger in numbers, we may prevent him from fighting. Scheme so as to discover his plans and the likelihood of their success.

23. Rouse him, and learn the principle of his activity or inactivity. Force him to reveal

himself, so as to find out his vulnerable spots.

24. Carefully compare the opposing army with your own, so that you may know where strength is superabundant and where it is deficient.

25. In making tactical dispositions, the highest pitch you can attain is to conceal them; conceal your dispositions, and you will be safe from the prying of the subtlest spies, from the machinations of the wisest brains.

26. How victory may be produced for them out of the enemy's own tactics that is what the multitude cannot comprehend.

27. All men can see the tactics whereby I conquer, but what none can see is the strategy out of which victory is evolved.

28. Do not repeat the tactics which have gained you one victory, but let your methods be regulated by the infinite variety of circumstances.

29. Military tactics are like unto water; for water in its natural course runs away from high places and hastens downwards.

30. So in war, the way is to avoid what is strong and to strike at what is weak.

31. Water shapes its course according to the nature of the ground over which it flows; the soldier works out his victory in relation to the foe whom he is facing.

32. Therefore, just as water retains no constant shape, so in warfare there are no constant conditions.

33. He who can modify his tactics in relation to his opponent and thereby succeed in winning, may be called a heaven-born captain.

34. The five elements (water, fire, wood, metal, earth) are not always equally predominant; the four seasons make way for each other in turn. There are short days and long; the moon has its periods of waning and waxing.

VII. Maneuvering

1. Sun Tzu said: In war, the general receives his commands from the sovereign.

2. Having collected an army and concentrated his forces, he must blend and harmonize the different elements thereof before pitching his camp.

3. After that, comes tactical maneuvering, than which there is nothing more difficult. The difficulty of tactical maneuvering consists in turning the devious into the direct, and misfortune into gain.

4. Thus, to take a long and circuitous route, after enticing the enemy out of the way, and though starting after him, to contrive to reach the goal before him, shows knowledge of the artifice of DEVIATION.

5. Maneuvering with an army is advantageous; with an undisciplined multitude, most dangerous.

6. If you set a fully equipped army in march in order to snatch an advantage, the chances are that you will be too late. On the other hand, to detach a flying column for the purpose involves the sacrifice of its baggage and stores.

7. Thus, if you order your men to roll up their buff-coats, and make forced marches

without halting day or night, covering double the usual distance at a stretch, doing a hundred LI in order to wrest an advantage, the leaders of all your three divisions will fall into the hands of the enemy.

Stonewall Jackson said: "The hardships of forced marches are often more painful than the dangers of battle." He did not often call upon his troops for extraordinary exertions. It was only when he intended a surprise, or when a rapid retreat was imperative, that he sacrificed everything for speed. ("Stonewall Jackson," *vol. I, p. 421*)

8. The stronger men will be in front, the jaded ones will fall behind, and on this plan only one-tenth of your army will reach its destination.

9. If you march fifty LI (one-third mile) in order to outmaneuver the enemy, you will lose the leader of your first division, and only half your force will reach the goal.

10. If you march thirty LI with the same object, two-thirds of your army will arrive.

11. We may take it then that an army without its baggage-train is lost; without provisions it is lost; without bases of supply it is lost.

12. We cannot enter into alliances until we are acquainted with the designs of our neighbors.

13. We are not fit to lead an army on the march unless we are familiar with the face of the country its mountains and forests, its pitfalls and precipices, its marshes and swamps.

14. We shall be unable to turn natural advantage to account unless we make use of local guides.

15. In war, practice dissimulation, and you will succeed.

16. Whether to concentrate or to divide your troops, must be decided by circumstances.

17. Let your rapidity be that of the wind, your compactness that of the forest.

18. In raiding and plundering be like fire, be immovability like a mountain.

19. Let your plans be dark and impenetrable as night, and when you move, fall like a thunderbolt.

20. When you plunder a countryside, let the spoil be divided amongst your men; when you capture new territory, cut it up into allotments for the benefit of the soldiery.

21. Ponder and deliberate before you make a move.

22. He will conquer who has learnt the artifice of deviation. Such is the art of maneuvering.

23. The Book of Army Management says: On the field of battle, the spoken word does not carry far enough: hence the institution of gongs and drums. Nor can ordinary objects be seen clearly enough: hence the institution of banners and flags.

24. Gongs and drums, banners and flags, are means whereby the ears and eyes of the host may be focused on one particular point.

25. The host thus forming a single united body, is it impossible either for the brave to

advance alone, or for the cowardly to retreat alone. This is the art of handling large masses of men.

26. In night-fighting, then, make much use of signal-fires and drums, and in fighting by day, of flags and banners, as a means of influencing the ears and eyes of your army.

27. A whole army may be robbed of its spirit; a commander-in-chief may be robbed of his presence of mind.

28. Now a solider's spirit is keenest in the morning; by noonday it has begun to flag; and in the evening, his mind is bent only on returning to camp.

29. A clever general, therefore, avoids an army when its spirit is keen, but attacks it when it is sluggish and inclined to return. This is the art of studying moods.

30. Disciplined and calm, to await the appearance of disorder and hubbub amongst the enemy: this is the art of retaining self-possession.

31. To be near the goal while the enemy is still far from it, to wait at ease while the enemy

is toiling and struggling, to be well-fed while the enemy is famished: this is the art of husbanding one's strength.

32. To refrain from intercepting an enemy whose banners are in perfect order, to refrain from attacking an army drawn up in calm and confident array: this is the art of studying circumstances.

33. It is a military axiom not to advance uphill against the enemy, nor to oppose him when he comes downhill.

34. Do not pursue an enemy who simulates flight; do not attack soldiers whose temper is keen.

35. Do not swallow bait offered by the enemy. Do not interfere with an army that is returning home.

36. When you surround an army, leave an outlet free. Do not press a desperate foe too hard.

37. Such is the *Art of War*fare.

VIII. Variations in Tactics

1. Sun Tzu said: In war, the general receives his commands from the sovereign, collects his army and concentrates his forces.

2. When in difficult country, do not encamp. In country where high roads intersect, join hands with your allies. Do not linger in dangerously isolated positions. In hemmed-in situations, you must resort to stratagem. In desperate position, you must fight.

3. There are roads which must not be followed, armies which must be not attacked, towns which must not be besieged, positions which must not be contested, commands of the sovereign which must not be obeyed.

4. The general who thoroughly understands the advantages that accompany variation of tactics knows how to handle his troops.

5. The general who does not understand these, may be well acquainted with the configuration of the country, yet he will not be able to turn his knowledge to practical account.

6. So, the student of war who is unversed in the *Art of War* of varying his plans, even though he be acquainted with the Five Advantages, will fail to make the best use of his men.

7. Hence in the wise leader's plans, considerations of advantage and of disadvantage will be blended together.

8. If our expectation of advantage be tempered in this way, we may succeed in accomplishing the essential part of our schemes.

9. If, on the other hand, in the midst of difficulties we are always ready to seize an advantage, we may extricate ourselves from misfortune.

10. Reduce the hostile chiefs by inflicting damage on them; and make trouble for them, and keep them constantly engaged; hold out specious allurements, and make them rush to any given point.

11. The *Art of War* teaches us to rely not on the likelihood of the enemy's not coming, but on our own readiness to receive him; not on the chance of his not attacking, but

rather on the fact that we have made our position unassailable.

12. There are five dangerous faults which may affect a general: (1) Recklessness, which leads to destruction; (2) cowardice, which leads to capture; (3) a hasty temper, which can be provoked by insults; (4) a delicacy of honor which is sensitive to shame; (5) over-solicitude for his men, which exposes him to worry and trouble.

13. These are the five besetting sins of a general, ruinous to the conduct of war.

14. When an army is overthrown and its leader slain, the cause will surely be found among these five dangerous faults. Let them be a subject of meditation.

IX. The Army on the March

1. Sun Tzu said: We come now to the question of encamping the army, and observing signs of the enemy. Pass quickly over mountains, and keep in the neighborhood of valleys.

2. Camp in high places, facing the sun. Do not climb heights in order to fight. So much for mountain warfare.

3. After crossing a river, you should get far away from it.

4. When an invading force crosses a river in its onward march, do not advance to meet it in mid-stream. It will be best to let half the army get across, and then deliver your attack.

5. If you are anxious to fight, you should not go to meet the invader near a river which he has to cross.

6. Moor your craft higher up than the enemy, and facing the sun. Do not move up-stream to meet the enemy. So much for river warfare.

7. In crossing salt-marshes, your sole concern should be to get over them quickly, without any delay.

8. If forced to fight in a salt-marsh, you should have water and grass near you, and get your back to a clump of trees. So much for operations in salt-marches.

9. In dry, level country, take up an easily accessible position with rising ground to your right and on your rear, so that the danger may be in front, and safety lie behind. So much for campaigning in flat country.

10. These are the four useful branches of military knowledge which enabled the Yellow Emperor to vanquish four several sovereigns.

11. All armies prefer high ground to low, and sunny places to dark.

12. If you are careful of your men, and camp on hard ground, the army will be free from disease of every kind, and this will spell victory.

13. When you come to a hill or a bank, occupy the sunny side, with the slope on your right rear. Thus you will at once act for the benefit of your soldiers and utilize the natural advantages of the ground.

14. When, in consequence of heavy rains up-country, a river which you wish to ford is swollen and flecked with foam, you must wait until it subsides.

15. Country in which there are precipitous cliffs with torrents running between, deep natural hollows, confined places, tangled thickets, quagmires and crevasses, should be left with all possible speed and not approached.

16. While we keep away from such places, we should get the enemy to approach them; while we face them, we should let the enemy have them on his rear.

17. If in the neighborhood of your camp there should be any hilly country, ponds surrounded by aquatic grass, hollow basins filled with reeds, or woods with thick undergrowth, they must be carefully routed out and searched; for these are places where men in ambush or insidious spies are likely to be lurking.

18. When the enemy is close at hand and remains quiet, he is relying on the natural strength of his position.

19. When he keeps aloof and tries to provoke a battle, he is anxious for the other side to advance.

20. If his place of encampment is easy of access, he is tendering a bait.

21. Movement amongst the trees of a forest shows that the enemy is advancing. The appearance of a number of screens in the midst of thick grass means that the enemy wants to make us suspicious.

22. The rising of birds in their flight is the sign of an ambuscade. Startled beasts indicate that a sudden attack is coming.

23. When there is dust rising in a high column, it is the sign of chariots advancing; when the dust is low, but spread over a wide area, it betokens the approach of infantry. When it branches out in different directions, it shows that parties have been sent to collect firewood. A few clouds of dust moving to and fro signify that the army is encamping.

24. Humble words and increased preparations are signs that the enemy is about to advance. Violent language and driving forward as if to the attack are signs that he will retreat.

25. When the light chariots come out first and take up a position on the wings, it is a sign that the enemy is forming for battle.

26. Peace proposals unaccompanied by a sworn covenant indicate a plot.

27. When there is much running about and the soldiers fall into rank, it means that the critical moment has come.

28. When some are seen advancing and some retreating, it is a lure.

29. When the soldiers stand leaning on their spears, they are faint from want of food.

30. If those who are sent to draw water begin by drinking themselves, the army is suffering from thirst.

31. If the enemy sees an advantage to be gained and makes no effort to secure it, the soldiers are exhausted.

32. If birds gather on any spot, it is unoccupied. Clamor by night betokens nervousness.

33. If there is disturbance in the camp, the general's authority is weak. If the banners

and flags are shifted about, sedition is afoot. If the officers are angry, it means that the men are weary.

34. When an army feeds its horses with grain and kills its cattle for food, and when the men do not hang their cooking-pots over the camp-fires, showing that they will not return to their tents, you may know that they are determined to fight to the death.

35. The sight of men whispering together in small knots or speaking in subdued tones points to disaffection amongst the rank and file.

36. Too frequent rewards signify that the enemy is at the end of his resources; too many punishments betray a condition of dire distress.

37. To begin by bluster, but afterwards to take fright at the enemy's numbers, shows a supreme lack of intelligence.

38. When envoys are sent with compliments in their mouths, it is a sign that the enemy wishes for a truce.

39. If the enemy's troops march up angrily and remain facing ours for a long time without either joining battle or taking themselves off again, the situation is one that demands great vigilance and circumspection.

40. If our troops are no more in number than the enemy, that is amply sufficient; it only means that no direct attack can be made. What we can do is simply to concentrate all our available strength, keep a close watch on the enemy, and obtain reinforcements.

41. He who exercises no forethought but makes light of his opponents is sure to be captured by them.

42. If soldiers are punished before they have grown attached to you, they will not prove submissive; and, unless submissive, then will be practically useless. If, when the soldiers have become attached to you, punishments are not enforced, they will still be unless.

43. Therefore soldiers must be treated in the first instance with humanity, but kept under control by means of iron discipline. This is a certain road to victory.

44. If in training soldiers commands are habitually enforced, the army will be well-disciplined; if not, its discipline will be bad.

45. If a general shows confidence in his men but always insists on his orders being obeyed, the gain will be mutual.

X. Terrain

1. Sun Tzu said: We may distinguish six kinds of terrain, to wit: (1) Accessible ground; (2) entangling ground; (3) temporizing ground; (4) narrow passes; (5) precipitous heights; (6) positions at a great distance from the enemy.

2. Ground which can be freely traversed by both sides is called ACCESSIBLE.

3. Give regard to ground of this nature, be before the enemy in occupying the raised and sunny spots, and carefully guard your

line of supplies. Then you will be able to fight with advantage.

4. Ground which can be abandoned but is hard to reoccupy is called ENTANGLING.

5. From a position of this sort, if the enemy is unprepared, you may sally forth and defeat him. But if the enemy is prepared for your coming, and you fail to defeat him, then, return being impossible, disaster will ensue.

6. When the position is such that neither side will gain by making the first move, it is called TEMPORIZING ground.

7. In a position of this sort, even though the enemy should offer us an attractive bait, it will be advisable not to stir forth, but rather to retreat, thus enticing the enemy in his turn; then, when part of his army has come out, we may deliver our attack with advantage.

8. With regard to NARROW PASSES, if you can occupy them first, let them be strongly garrisoned and await the advent of the enemy.

9. Should the army forestall you in occupying a pass, do not go after him if the pass is fully garrisoned, but only if it is weakly garrisoned.

10. With regard to PRECIPITOUS HEIGHTS, if you are beforehand with your adversary, you should occupy the raised and sunny spots, and there wait for him to come up.

11. If the enemy has occupied them before you, do not follow him, but retreat and try to entice him away.

12. If you are situated at a great distance from the enemy, and the strength of the two armies is equal, it is not easy to provoke a battle, and fighting will be to your disadvantage.

13. These six are the principles connected with Earth. The general who has attained a responsible post must be careful to study them.

14. Now an army is exposed to six several calamities, not arising from natural causes, but from faults for which the general is responsible. These are: (1) Flight; (2)

insubordination; (3) collapse; (4) ruin; (5) disorganization; (6) rout.

15. Other conditions being equal, if one force is hurled against another ten times its size, the result will be the FLIGHT of the former.

16. When the common soldiers are too strong and their officers too weak, the result is INSUBORDINATION. When the officers are too strong and the common soldiers too weak, the result is COLLAPSE.

17. When the higher officers are angry and insubordinate, and on meeting the enemy give battle on their own account from a feeling of resentment, before the commander-in-chief can tell whether or not he is in a position to fight, the result is RUIN.

18. When the general is weak and without authority; when his orders are not clear and distinct; when there are no fixed duties assigned to officers and men, and the ranks are formed in a slovenly haphazard manner, the result is utter DISORGANIZATION.

19. When a general, unable to estimate the enemy's strength, allows an inferior force to engage a larger one, or hurls a weak detachment against a powerful one, and neglects to place picked soldiers in the front rank, the result must be ROUT.

20. These are six ways of courting defeat, which must be carefully noted by the general who has attained a responsible post.

21. The natural formation of the country is the soldier's best ally; but a power of estimating the adversary, of controlling the forces of victory, and of shrewdly calculating difficulties, dangers and distances, constitutes the test of a great general.

22. He who knows these things, and in fighting puts his knowledge into practice, will win his battles. He who knows them not, nor practices them, will surely be defeated.

23. If fighting is sure to result in victory, then you must fight, even though the ruler forbid it; if fighting will not result in victory,

then you must not fight even at the ruler's bidding.

24. The general who advances without coveting fame and retreats without fearing disgrace, whose only thought is to protect his country and do good service for his sovereign, is the jewel of the kingdom.

25. Regard your soldiers as your children, and they will follow you into the deepest valleys; look upon them as your own beloved sons, and they will stand by you even unto death.

26. If, however, you are indulgent, but unable to make your authority felt; kind-hearted, but unable to enforce your commands; and incapable, moreover, of quelling disorder: then your soldiers must be likened to spoilt children; they are useless for any practical purpose.

27. If we know that our own men are in a condition to attack, but are unaware that the enemy is not open to attack, we have gone only halfway towards victory.

28. If we know that the enemy is open to attack, but are unaware that our own men

are not in a condition to attack, we have gone only halfway towards victory.

29. If we know that the enemy is open to attack, and also know that our men are in a condition to attack, but are unaware that the nature of the ground makes fighting impracticable, we have still gone only halfway towards victory.

30. Hence the experienced soldier, once in motion, is never bewildered; once he has broken camp, he is never at a loss.

31. Hence the saying: If you know the enemy and know yourself, your victory will not stand in doubt; if you know Heaven and know Earth, you may make your victory complete.

XI. *The Nine Situations*

1. Sun Tzu said: The *Art of War* recognizes nine varieties of ground: (1) Dispersive ground; (2) facile ground; (3) contentious ground; (4) open ground; (5) ground of intersecting highways; (6) serious ground;

(7) difficult ground; (8) hemmed-in ground; (9) desperate ground.

2. When a chieftain is fighting in his own territory, it is dispersive ground.

3. When he has penetrated into hostile territory, but to no great distance, it is facile ground.

4. Ground the possession of which imports great advantage to either side, is contentious ground.

5. Ground on which each side has liberty of movement is open ground.

6. Ground which forms the key to three contiguous states, so that he who occupies it first has most of the Empire at his command, is a ground of intersecting highways.

7. When an army has penetrated into the heart of a hostile country, leaving a number of fortified cities in its rear, it is serious ground.

8. Mountain forests, rugged steeps, marshes and fens all country that is hard to traverse: this is difficult ground.

9. Ground which is reached through narrow gorges, and from which we can only retire by tortuous paths, so that a small number of the enemy would suffice to crush a large body of our men: this is hemmed in ground.

10. Ground on which we can only be saved from destruction by fighting without delay, is desperate ground.

11. On dispersive ground, therefore, fight not. On facile ground, halt not. On contentious ground, attack not.

12. On open ground, do not try to block the enemy's way. On the ground of intersecting highways, join hands with your allies.

13. On serious ground, gather in plunder. In difficult ground, keep steadily on the march.

14. On hemmed-in ground, resort to stratagem. On desperate ground, fight.

15. Those who were called skillful leaders of old knew how to drive a wedge between the enemy's front and rear; to prevent co-operation between his large and small

divisions; to hinder the good troops from rescuing the bad, the officers from rallying their men.

16. When the enemy's men were united, they managed to keep them in disorder.

17. When it was to their advantage, they made a forward move; when otherwise, they stopped still.

18. If asked how to cope with a great host of the enemy in orderly array and on the point of marching to the attack, I should say: "Begin by seizing something which your opponent holds dear; then he will be amenable to your will."

19. Rapidity is the essence of war: take advantage of the enemy's unreadiness, make your way by unexpected routes, and attack unguarded spots.

20. The following are the principles to be observed by an invading force: The further you penetrate into a country, the greater will be the solidarity of your troops, and thus the defenders will not prevail against you.

21. Make forays in fertile country in order to supply your army with food.

22. Carefully study the well-being of your men, and do not overtax them. Concentrate your energy and hoard your strength. Keep your army continually on the move, and devise unfathomable plans.

23. Throw your soldiers into positions whence there is no escape, and they will prefer death to flight. If they will face death, there is nothing they may not achieve. Officers and men alike will put forth their uttermost strength.

24. Soldiers when in desperate straits lose the sense of fear. If there is no place of refuge, they will stand firm. If they are in hostile country, they will show a stubborn front. If there is no help for it, they will fight hard.

25. Thus, without waiting to be marshaled, the soldiers will be constantly on the qui vive; without waiting to be asked, they will do your will; without restrictions, they will be faithful; without giving orders, they can be trusted.

26. Prohibit the taking of omens, and do away with superstitious doubts. Then, until death itself comes, no calamity need be feared.

27. If our soldiers are not overburdened with money, it is not because they have a distaste for riches; if their lives are not unduly long, it is not because they are disinclined to longevity.

28. On the day they are ordered out to battle, your soldiers may weep, those sitting up bedewing their garments, and those lying down letting the tears run down their cheeks. But let them once be brought to bay, and they will display the courage of a Chu or a Kuei (forest demon).

29. The skillful tactician may be likened to the SHUAIJAN. Now the SHUAI-JAN is a snake that is found in the Ch`ang mountains. Strike at its head, and you will be attacked by its tail; strike at its tail, and you will be attacked by its head; strike at its middle, and you will be attacked by head and tail both.

30. Asked if an army can be made to imitate the SHUAIJAN, I should answer, Yes. For the men of Wu and the men of Yueh are enemies; yet if they are crossing a river in the same boat and are caught by a storm, they will come to each other's assistance just as the left hand helps the right.

31. Hence it is not enough to put one's trust in the tethering of horses, and the burying of chariot wheels in the ground.

32. The principle on which to manage an army is to set up one standard of courage which all must reach.

33. How to make the best of both strong and weak, that is a question involving the proper use of ground.

34. Thus the skillful general conducts his army just as though he were leading a single man, willy-nilly, by the hand.

35. It is the business of a general to be quiet and thus ensure secrecy; upright and just, and thus maintain order.

36. He must be able to mystify his officers and men by false reports and appearances, and thus keep them in total ignorance.

37. By altering his arrangements and changing his plans, he keeps the enemy without definite knowledge. By shifting his camp and taking circuitous routes, he prevents the enemy from anticipating his purpose.

38. At the critical moment, the leader of an army acts like one who has climbed up a height and then kicks away the ladder behind him. He carries his men deep into hostile territory before he shows his hand.

39. He burns his boats and breaks his cooking-pots; like a shepherd driving a flock of sheep, he drives his men this way and that, and nothing knows whither he is going.

40. To muster his host and bring it into danger: this may be termed the business of the general.

41. The different measures suited to the nine varieties of ground; the expediency of aggressive or defensive tactics; and the fundamental laws of human nature: these

are things that must most certainly be studied.

42. When invading hostile territory, the general principle is, that penetrating deeply brings cohesion; penetrating but a short way means dispersion.

43. When you leave your own country behind, and take your army across neighborhood territory, you find yourself on critical ground. When there are means of communication on all four sides, the ground is one of intersecting highways.

44. When you penetrate deeply into a country, it is serious ground. When you penetrate but a little way, it is facile ground.

45. When you have the enemy's strongholds on your rear, and narrow passes in front, it is hemmed-in ground. When there is no place of refuge at all, it is desperate ground.

46. Therefore, on dispersive ground, I would inspire my men with unity of purpose. On facile ground, I would see that there is close connection between all parts of my army.

47. On contentious ground, I would hurry up my rear.

48. On open ground, I would keep a vigilant eye on my defenses. On ground of intersecting highways, I would consolidate my alliances.

49. On serious ground, I would try to ensure a continuous stream of supplies. On difficult ground, I would keep pushing on along the road.

50. On hemmed-in ground, I would block any way of retreat. On desperate ground, I would proclaim to my soldiers the hopelessness of saving their lives.

51. For it is the soldier's disposition to offer an obstinate resistance when surrounded, to fight hard when he cannot help himself, and to obey promptly when he has fallen into danger.

52. We cannot enter into alliance with neighboring princes until we are acquainted with their designs. We are not fit to lead an army on the march unless we are familiar with the face of the country its mountains and forests, its pitfalls and

precipices, its marshes and swamps. We shall be unable to turn natural advantages to account unless we make use of local guides.

53. To be ignored of any one of the following four or five principles does not befit a warlike prince.

54. When a warlike prince attacks a powerful state, his generalship shows itself in preventing the concentration of the enemy's forces. He overawes his opponents, and their allies are prevented from joining against him.

55. Hence he does not strive to ally himself with all and sundry, nor does he foster the power of other states. He carries out his own secret designs, keeping his antagonists in awe. Thus he is able to capture their cities and overthrow their kingdoms.

56. Bestow rewards without regard to rule, issue orders without regard to previous arrangements; and you will be able to handle a whole army as though you had to do with but a single man.

57. Confront your soldiers with the deed itself; never let them know your design. When the outlook is bright, bring it before their eyes; but tell them nothing when the situation is gloomy.

58. Place your army in deadly peril, and it will survive; plunge it into desperate straits, and it will come off in safety.

59. For it is precisely when a force has fallen into harm's way that is capable of striking a blow for victory.

60. Success in warfare is gained by carefully accommodating ourselves to the enemy's purpose.

61. By persistently hanging on the enemy's flank, we shall succeed in the long run in killing the commander-in-chief.

62. This is called ability to accomplish a thing by sheer cunning.

63. On the day that you take up your command, block the frontier passes, destroy the official tallies, and stop the passage of all emissaries.

64. Be stern in the council-chamber, so that you may control the situation.

65. If the enemy leaves a door open, you must rush in.

66. Forestall your opponent by seizing what he holds dear, and subtly contrive to time his arrival on the ground.

67. Walk in the path defined by rule, and accommodate yourself to the enemy until you can fight a decisive battle.

68. At first, then, exhibit the coyness of a maiden, until the enemy gives you an opening; afterwards emulate the rapidity of a running hare, and it will be too late for the enemy to oppose you.

XII. The Attack by Fire

1. Sun Tzu said: There are five ways of attacking with fire. The first is to burn soldiers in their camp; the second is to burn stores; the third is to burn baggage trains;

the fourth is to burn arsenals and magazines; the fifth is to hurl dropping fire amongst the enemy.

2. In order to carry out an attack, we must have means available. The material for raising fire should always be kept in readiness.

3. There is a proper season for making attacks with fire, and special days for starting a conflagration.

4. The proper season is when the weather is very dry; the special days are those when the moon is in the constellations of the Sieve, the Wall, the Wing or the Cross-bar; for these four are all days of rising wind.

5. In attacking with fire, one should be prepared to meet five possible developments:

6. (1) When fire breaks out inside to enemy's camp, respond at once with an attack from without.

7. (2) If there is an outbreak of fire, but the enemy's soldiers remain quiet, bide your time and do not attack.

8. (3) When the force of the flames has reached its height, follow it up with an attack, if that is practicable; if not, stay where you are.

9. (4) If it is possible to make an assault with fire from without, do not wait for it to break out within, but deliver your attack at a favorable moment.

10. (5) When you start a fire, be to windward of it. Do not attack from the leeward.

11. A wind that rises in the daytime lasts long, but a night breeze soon falls.

12. In every army, the five developments connected with fire must be known, the movements of the stars calculated, and a watch kept for the proper days.

13. Hence those who use fire as an aid to the attack show intelligence; those who use water as an aid to the attack gain an accession of strength.

14. By means of water, an enemy may be intercepted, but not robbed of all his belongings.

15. Unhappy is the fate of one who tries to win his battles and succeed in his attacks without cultivating the spirit of enterprise; for the result is waste of time and general stagnation.

16. Hence the saying: The enlightened ruler lays his plans well ahead; the good general cultivates his resources.

17. Move not unless you see an advantage; use not your troops unless there is something to be gained; fight not unless the position is critical.

18. No ruler should put troops into the field merely to gratify his own spleen; no general should fight a battle simply out of pique.

19. If it is to your advantage, make a forward move; if not, stay where you are.

20. Anger may in time change to gladness; vexation may be succeeded by content.

21. But a kingdom that has once been destroyed can never come again into being; nor can the dead ever be brought back to life.

22. Hence the enlightened ruler is heedful, and the good general full of caution. This is the way to keep a country at peace and an army intact.

XIII. The Use of Spies

1. Sun Tzu said: Raising a host of a hundred thousand men and marching them great distances entails heavy loss on the people and a drain on the resources of the State. The daily expenditure will amount to a thousand ounces of silver. There will be commotion at home and abroad, and men will drop down exhausted on the highways. As many as seven hundred thousand families will be impeded in their labor.

2. Hostile armies may face each other for years, striving for the victory which is decided in a single day. This being so, to remain in ignorance of the enemy's condition simply because one grudges the outlay of a hundred ounces of silver in honors and emoluments, is the height of inhumanity.

3. One who acts thus is no leader of men, no present help to his sovereign, no master of victory.

4. Thus, what enables the wise sovereign and the good general to strike and conquer, and achieve things beyond the reach of ordinary men, is FOREKNOWLEDGE.

5. Now this foreknowledge cannot be elicited from spirits; it cannot be obtained inductively from experience, nor by any deductive calculation.

6. Knowledge of the enemy's dispositions can only be obtained from other men.

7. Hence the use of spies, of whom there are five classes: (1) Local spies; (2) inward spies; (3) converted spies; (4) doomed spies; (5) surviving spies.

8. When these five kinds of spy are all at work, none can discover the secret system. This is called "divine manipulation of the threads." It is the sovereign's most precious faculty.

9. Having LOCAL SPIES means employing the services of the inhabitants of a district.

10. Having INWARD SPIES, making use of officials of the enemy.

11. Having CONVERTED SPIES, getting hold of the enemy's spies and using them for our own purposes.

12. Having DOOMED SPIES, doing certain things openly for purposes of deception, and allowing our spies to know of them and report them to the enemy.

13. SURVIVING SPIES, finally, are those who bring back news from the enemy's camp.

14. Hence it is that which none in the whole army are more intimate relations to be maintained than with spies. None should be more liberally rewarded. In no other business should greater secrecy be preserved.

15. Spies cannot be usefully employed without a certain intuitive sagacity.

16. They cannot be properly managed without benevolence and straightforwardness.

17. Without subtle ingenuity of mind, one cannot make certain of the truth of their reports.

18. Be subtle! be subtle! and use your spies for every kind of business.

19. If a secret piece of news is divulged by a spy before the time is ripe, he must be put to death together with the man to whom the secret was told.

20. Whether the object be to crush an army, to storm a city, or to assassinate an individual, it is always necessary to begin by finding out the names of the attendants, the aides-de-camp, and door-keepers and sentries of the general in command. Our spies must be commissioned to ascertain these.

21. The enemy's spies who have come to spy on us must be sought out, tempted with bribes, led away and comfortably housed. Thus they will become converted spies and available for our service.

22. It is through the information brought by the converted spy that we are able to acquire and employ local and inward spies.

23. It is owing to his information, again, that we can cause the doomed spy to carry false tidings to the enemy.

24. Lastly, it is by his information that the surviving spy can be used on appointed occasions.

25. The end and aim of spying in all its five varieties is knowledge of the enemy; and this knowledge can only be derived, in the first instance, from the converted spy. Hence it is essential that the converted spy be treated with the utmost liberality.

26. Of old, the rise of the Yin dynasty was due to I Chih who had served under the Hsia. Likewise, the rise of the Chou dynasty was due to Lu Ya who had served under the Yin.

27. Hence it is only the enlightened ruler and the wise general who will use the highest intelligence of the army for purposes of spying and thereby they achieve great results. Spies are a most important element in water, because on them depends an army's ability to move.

The Book of Mormon's Art of War (24 Additional Principles)

What is 'the Strength of the Lord'?

The *Strength of the Lord* is nothing less than God's infinite power—a strength and force which nothing else has ever matched, does now match, or will match in the future. It is utter foolishness to compare any other power with this omnipotent strength. As Nephi said to Laman and Lemuel, after the later two expressed a greater confidence in Laban and those under his command, "...for behold, he [God] is mightier than all the earth, then why not mightier than Laban and his fifty, yea, or even than his tens of thousands?"

We can gain much insight into the *strength of the Lord* by, in detail, observing the character of one man—Captain Moroni, for the scriptures say:

> And Moroni was a strong and a mighty man; he was a man of a perfect understanding; yea, a man that did not delight in bloodshed; a man whose soul did joy in the liberty and the freedom of his country, and his brethren from

bondage and slavery; Yea, a man whose heart did swell with thanksgiving to his God, for the many privileges and blessings which he bestowed upon his people; a man who did labor exceedingly for the welfare and safety of his people. Yea, and he was a man who was firm in the faith of Christ, and he had sworn with an oath to defend his people, his rights, and his country, and his religion, even to the loss of his blood.

Now the Nephites were taught to defend themselves against their enemies, even to the shedding of blood if it were necessary; yea, and they were also taught never to give an offense, yea, and never to raise the sword except it were against an enemy, except it were to preserve their lives.

And this was their faith, that by so doing God would prosper them in the land, or in other words, if they were faithful in keeping the commandments of God that he would prosper them in the land; yea, warn them to flee, or to prepare for war, according to their danger; And also, that God would make it known unto them whither they should go to defend themselves against their enemies, and by so doing, the Lord would deliver them; and this was the faith of Moroni, and his heart did glory in it; not in the shedding of blood but in doing good, in preserving his people, yea, in keeping the commandments of God, yea, and resisting iniquity.

Yea, verily, verily I say unto you, if all men had been, and were, and ever would be, like unto Moroni, behold, the very powers of hell would have been shaken forever; yea, the devil would never have power over the hearts of the children of men.

Behold, he was a man like unto Ammon, the son of Mosiah, yea, and even the other sons of Mosiah, yea, and also Alma and his sons, for they were all men of God. (Alma 48:11-18)

Along with Moroni being described for his patriotism, it is poignant that he is also described as a man like unto Ammon and his confidants, men who:

...had waxed strong in the knowledge of the truth; for they were men [also] of a sound understanding [because] they had searched the scriptures diligently, that they might know the word of God. But this is not all; they had given themselves to much prayer, and fasting; therefore they had the spirit of prophecy, and the spirit of revelation, and when they taught, they taught with power and authority of God. (Alma 17:2-3)

Principle 1 in the Book of Mormon's *Art of War* is:

Fighting "in the strength of the Lord" will always end in victory; without the Strength of the Lord, the Wicked destroy the Wicked, and Victory is decided by the Strength and Cunning of Man

When Moroni's soldiers had sufficiently surrounded Zerahemnah and his wicked army of Lamanites, he ordered a halt to the massacre his army was inflicting, and withdrew a pace from them. Moroni then expressed to Zerahemnah Principle 1 of The Book of Mormon's *Art of War*:

> ...ye behold that the Lord is with us; and ye behold that he has delivered you into our hands. And now I would that ye should understand that this is done unto us because of our religion and our faith in Christ. And now ye see that ye cannot destroy this our faith. Now ye see that this is the true faith of God; yea, ye see that God will support, and keep, and preserve us, so long as we are faithful unto him, and unto our faith, and our religion; and never will the Lord suffer that we shall be destroyed except we should fall into transgression and deny our faith. (Alma 44:3-4)

Yet when the wicked battle the wicked, the Lord withdraws His strength and both aggressors become weakly dependent on their own might, as explained by Mormon:

> And it came to pass that when they had fled we did pursue them with our armies, and did meet them again, and did beat them; nevertheless *the strength of the Lord* was not with us; yea, we were left to ourselves, that the Spirit of the Lord did not abide in us;

> therefore we had become weak like unto our brethren. (Mormon 2:26)

The beginning of 1787 Constitutional Convention was a time of adversity and distrust among the delegates who met in Philadelphia. It was during the peak of animosity when Benjamin Franklin stood up and gave his legendary plea for prayer. Much of what was said applies to Principle 1 of The Book of Mormon's Art of War. He said, in part:

> "I have lived, Sir, a long time, and the longer I live, the more convincing proofs I see of this truth—that God governs in the affairs of men. And if a sparrow cannot fall to the ground without His notice, is it probable that an empire can rise without His aid? We have been assured, Sir, in the sacred writings, that "except the Lord build the House they labour in vain that build it." I firmly believe this; and I also believe that without his concurring aid we shall succeed in this political building no better than the Builders of Babel: We shall be divided by our little partial local interests; our projects will be confounded, and we ourselves shall become a reproach and bye word down

to future ages. And what is worse, mankind may hereafter from this unfortunate instance, despair of establishing Governments by human wisdom and leave it to *chance, war and conquest*. (Taken from James Madison's notes, year 1787, edited slightly for punctuation)

Chance in war and conquest can be expected when one goes NOT out *In the Strength of the Lord*.

As an added caveat to this principle, the Lord many times allows defeat to that army where greater expectations have been afforded. As related by Elder Bruce R. McKonkie in the chapter heading of Alma 53, "Dissensions among the Nephites [those with the gospel] give rise to Lamanite victories." Such has been a pattern of the Lord in the entire cannon of scriptural accounts of wars.

Other scriptures affirming **Principle 1** include 1 Nephi 1:20, 1 Nephi 2:23, 1 Nephi 3:7, 1 Nephi 3:31-4:1, 2 Nephi 10:13, Mormon 9:21, Alma 46:18, Alma 50:22, Alma 53:8-9, Alma 57:26-27, Alma 58:37, Alma 59:11-12, Alma 60:15-16, Alma 61:15, Helaman 4:11-14, Helaman 4:25-26, Helaman 7:22-23, 3 Nephi 2:18, 3 Nephi 3:15, 3 Nephi 4:9-12, Mormon 1:16-17, Mormon 2:10, 13, 15, Mormon 3:9-10, Mormon 4:5,

Mormon 4:13, Mormon 5:2, Mormon 7:4, Psalms 127:1, Acts 5:38-39, story of Noah in Genesis 6-8.

Principle 2:

Those who Gain <u>The Strength of the Lord</u> must make a Covenant or Oath to "maintain their rights (liberty), and their religion (as Christians)." (Alma 46:20)

When Moroni could see the handprint of future tyranny upon his country he "rent his coat; and he took a piece thereof, and wrote upon it—In memory of our God, our religion, and freedom, and our peace, our wives, and our children—and he fastened it upon the end of a pole." (Alma 46:12)

He then, "bowed himself to the earth, and he prayed mightily unto his God for the blessings of liberty to rest upon his brethren, so long as there should a band of Christians remain to possess the land." (Alma 46:13) It was at this time that he rallied the troops by doing which may have seemed unpopular in this day:

> And... he went forth among the people, waving the rent part of his garment in the air, that all might see the writing which he had written upon the rent part, and crying with a loud voice, saying: Behold, whosoever will

> maintain this title upon the land, let them come forth in the strength of the Lord, and enter into a covenant that they will maintain their *rights*, and their *religion*, that the Lord God may bless them. (Alma 46:19-200

The effect of this was monumental! The people began rallying behind Moroni, entering into a covenant, until eventually Moroni had won the hearts of the majority of his countrymen. (see Alma 46:29)

These had all entered into a covenant, which was two-fold—maintain *Liberty* AND *Christianity*.

Today's military, politicians, and officers take a similar oath. The spirit of the oath embodies an affirmation of Christ through the Constitution, yet this meaning has been lost through time until today it is completely gone; yet not so in early America, nor in the Book of Mormon.

In a 1942 Conference Report, David O. McKay, Second Counselor in the First Presidency, remarked:

> The Constitution of this government was written by men who accepted Jesus Christ as the Savior of mankind. Let men and women in these United States then continue to keep their eyes

centered upon Him who ever shines as a Light to all the world. Men and women who live in America, "the land of Zion" (D&C 57:2; D&C 63:25), have a responsibility greater than that yet borne by any other people. Theirs is the duty, the obligation, to preserve not only the Constitution of the land but the Christian principles from which sprang that immortal document.

Today, covenants within Christian churches leave void the oath to maintain liberty, while civil oaths of freedom & country void the name of Christ, yet Moroni specifically, "prayed mightily unto his God for the blessings of liberty to rest upon his brethren, *so long as there should a band of Christians remain to possess the land."* (Alma 46:13)

One cannot be achieved without the other. Indeed, as Ezra Taft Benson mentioned, "The fight for freedom *cannot be divorced from the gospel."* (Our Immediate Responsibility, 1966)

In the Book of Mormon, the oath to preserve liberty included "a covenant... [to] not forsake the Lord their God; [and if they were to] be ashamed to take upon them the name of Christ, the Lord should rend them even as they had rent their garments." (Alma 46:21)

THIS is the oath every lover of liberty must make in order to preserve "...our religion, and freedom, and our peace, our wives, and our children."

In the Book of Mormon it was a serious matter to NOT take upon yourself this oath, as explained in Principle 6.

In the Book of Mormon, this oath was considered an ordinance, as described when Pahoran took office:

> Behold, it came to pass that the son of Nephihah was appointed to fill the judgment-seat, in the stead of his father; yea, he was appointed chief judge and governor over the people, with *an oath and sacred ordinance to judge righteously*, and to keep the peace and the freedom of the people, and to grant unto them their sacred privileges to worship the Lord their God, yea, to support and maintain the cause of God all his days, and to bring the wicked to justice according to their crime. (Alma 50:39)

(see all of Alma 46, Alma 53:17, and Alma 51:39; as well as Principles 6 and 23)

. . .

The remainder of the Book of Mormon's *Art of War* principles can be broken up into three categories; principles for *Entering, Engaging,* and *Exiting* war.

Entering War: Determining Your Enemy

Principle 3:

War is only Justified in the Defense of Life, Property, and Liberty, including the People's Rights of Religion, and this After all other Reasonable Efforts for Peace have been Pursued

Alma 43:45 tells us that the Nephites under Captain Moroni:

> ...were not fighting for monarchy nor power but they were fighting for their homes and their liberties, their wives and their children, and their all, yea, for their rites of worship and their church. (Alma 43:45)

Up to the point of entrance into a just war, a long, drawn out story should have already unfolded, much like the story of America's War of Independence, where all other efforts for peace by reason, educational, and petition means had been exhausted. Pahoran tells Moroni:

> ...let us resist evil, and whatsoever evil we cannot resist **with our words**... **let us resist them with our swords**, that we may retain our freedom, that we may rejoice in the great privilege of our church, and in the cause of our Redeemer and our God. (Alma 61:14)

Amalickiah, in the Book of Mormon, was a man of cunning device who drew great power from Satan in destroying the church of God while simultaneously destroying the foundation of the Nephites' liberty. (Alma 46:10) When this happened, there came a point in time when Moroni had had enough. The time for teaching and pleading with the membership of the church and others to NOT buy into Amalickiah's flatteries was over—he, Amalickiah, was becoming a threat not to be ignored if the people valued their liberty.

Moroni could see the future as one in which his beloved country would soon fall under tyranny rule unless there was a forceful intervention. If there were any who were righteous, if there were any who were NOT brainwashed to Amalickiah's deceit, if there were *any* true Saints in his midst, he had to rally them. Thus:

> ...it came to pass that he [Moroni] rent his coat; and he took a piece thereof, and wrote upon it—In memory of our God, our religion, and freedom, and our peace, our wives, and our children—and he fastened it upon the end of a pole. And he fastened on his head-plate, and his breastplate, and his shields, and girded on his armor about his loins; and he took the pole, which had on the end thereof his rent coat, (and he called it the title of liberty) and he bowed himself to the earth, and he prayed mightily unto his God for the blessings of liberty to rest upon his brethren, so long as there should a band of Christians remain to possess the land..." (Alma 46:12-13)

In the wars that commenced, the scriptures continue to reiterate the stance Moroni led, by warring only to "support their liberty, their lands, their wives, and their children, and their peace, and that they might live unto the Lord their God, and that they might maintain that which was called by their enemies the cause of Christians." (Alma 48:10) And this support never entailed being the aggressor, for:

> ...the Nephites were taught to defend themselves against their enemies, even to the shedding of blood if it were necessary; yea, and they were also taught never to give an offense, yea, and never to raise the sword except it were against an enemy, except it were to preserve their lives. (Alma 48:14)

Likewise, Helaman's 2000 stripling warriors held this position. For they said:

> ...behold our God is with us, and he will not suffer that we should fall; then let us go forth; *we would not slay our brethren if they would let us alone*; therefore let us go, lest they should overpower the army of Antipus. (Alma 56:46)

For a description of why our enemies go to battle, see Mosiah 10:12-17

Other scriptures reaffirming this principle include Alma 60:17, Alma 43:9-10, Alma 43:26, Alma 43:30,

Alma 43:45-47, Alma 44:5-6, Alma 54:13, 3 Nephi 3:20-21, Mormon 2:23, Mormon 4:4.

Principle 4:

"Inasmuch as ye are not guilty of the first offense, neither the second, ye shall not suffer yourselves to be slain by the hands of your enemies" (Alma 43:46)

The Lord Jesus tells us that were someone to "smite thee on thy right cheek," your Christian duty would be to "turn to him the other also." (Matthew 5:39) Although this is true with smiting and contending, it is NOT true when an enemy's intent is to cause death.

Scriptural scholars may point to the Sermon on the Mount, the story of the Anti-Nephi-Lehites' position of complete non-aggression, and/or D&C 98 to justify sitting back and taking no action when life, liberty and/or property are being taken away. D&C 98:23-31 gives specific instruction for when one "smites" another, teaching the doctrine of a patience non-response until the 3rd and even the 4th attack. Yet the attacks in this scriptural record do not pertain to issues of the taking of life—or unto bloodshed. They strictly mention *only* the word "smite", meaning "hit".

When someone hits you, they have not taken away your life, liberty, or property, and most times when a person shows a non-aggressive love in reply, the offender will cease their conduct (see principle 7), for "A soft answer turneth away wrath..." (Prov. 15:1) But you are ALWAYS justified in *defending* your life, your property, and your liberty. For:

> ...the Lord has said that: Ye shall defend your families even unto bloodshed. Therefore for this cause were the Nephites contending with the Lamanites, to defend themselves, and their families, and their lands [property], their country, and their rights, and their religion. (Alma 43:47)

Principle 4 still involves the spirit of patient non-aggression by reacting non-offensively to an enemy's first attempt to take away life, liberty, and/or property. This principle DOES, however, authorize an offensive strike if there is a second attempt. (Alma 43:46)

Seldom, if ever, does one nation attack another nation without first manifesting belligerent tendencies of some kind. When it comes to early proclamations of war from one nation to another, in modern day the Lord has told His Saints:

> And if any nation, tongue, or people should proclaim war against them, they should first lift a standard of peace unto that people, nation, or tongue; And if that people did not accept the offering of peace, neither the second nor the third time, they should bring these testimonies before the Lord; Then I, the Lord, would give unto them a commandment, and justify them in going out to battle against that nation, tongue, or people.
>
> And I, the Lord, would fight their battles, and their children's battles, and their children's children's, until they had avenged themselves on all their enemies, to the third and fourth generation. (D&C 98:34-37)

It is recorded that Pahoran himself, a righteous governor of the Nephites, was confused as to when he would be justified in taking arms with the intent to shed blood; for, after being counseled by Moroni he said, "...for I was somewhat worried concerning what we should do, whether it should be just in us to go against our brethren." (Alma 61:19)

The answer to 'when is the time right?' has the potential to neutralize many would-be patriots, who cry "while evils are sufferable," instead of "...when a long train of abuses." (Declaration of Independence) Such will be hesitant to take up arms, as was Pahoran, when right reason warrants it. This author hopes men of today have the discernment of Moroni, and NOT be passive, timidly wondering when the threshold level of abuses has been reached.

Other scriptures reaffirming this principle include Alma 48:24-25, Alma 54:13, Alma 55:3, Alma 61:10-13, 3 Nephi 12:39-45, 4th Nephi 1:34.

Principle 5 (closely related to Principle 6):

"The inward vessel shall be cleansed first... even the great head of our government." (Alma 60:23-24)

Alma 60 is Moroni's epistle to Pahoran, the Chief Judge and Governor of the land. In this epistle, Moroni suspects Pahoran of not only purposefully neglecting the sending of provisions to his armies, but of seeking for power and authority over the people, much like the Lamanite army he is already fighting. For he writes to Pahoran saying, "We know not but what ye are also traitors to your country." (Alma 60:18)

As it turns out, Pahoran was holding true to the title of liberty, though dealing himself with insurrections of a people that ought to have supported him and the cause. One may wonder why Mormon, the primary abridger of the Book of Mormon, would choose to include a long and presumptuous accusation, as scripture. Yet this entire chapter gives us, today, wonderful insight into principle 5 of the Book of Mormon's *Art of War*—that of cleansing the inward vessel first, "even the great head of our government." This means that insurrections of those who support liberty are just, when directed towards a government which has become tyrannical. This means 'when injustice becomes law, rebellion becomes duty.' (Thomas Jefferson) Moroni was ready to turn on the leaders of his government, saying:

> And I will come unto you, and if there be any among you that has a desire for freedom, yea, if there be even a spark of freedom remaining, behold I will stir up insurrections among you, even until those who have desires to usurp power and authority shall become extinct. Yea, behold **I do not fear your power nor your authority**, but it is my God

whom I fear; and it is according to his commandments that I do take my sword to defend the cause of my country, and it is because of your iniquity that we have suffered so much loss.

Behold it is time, yea, the time is now at hand, that except ye do bestir yourselves in the defence of your country and your little ones, the sword of justice doth hang over you… behold, I come unto you, even in the land of Zarahemla, and smite you with the sword, insomuch that ye can have no more power to impede the progress of this people in the cause of our freedom. (Alma 60:27-30)

But wait! *Doesn't this position violate Doctrine & Covenants 134:1*, which states, "We believe that governments were instituted of God for the benefit of man…"

On this subject, Elder Erastus Snow, one of the twelve Apostles of the 19th century, and a leading figure in the Mormon colonization of the Western U.S., explains beautifully the doctrine of 'good, better, best' among world governments:

"Anarchy—shall I say, is the worst of all governments? No: Anarchy is the absence of all government; it is the antipodes [opposite] of order; it is the acme of confusion; it is the result of unbridled license, the antipodes of true liberty. The Apostle Paul says truly: 'For there is no power but of God: the powers that be are ordained of God.' At first this is a startling statement. Even the monopoly of the one-man-power as in Russia [the Czar], or the monopoly of the aristocracy as in other parts of Europe, or the imbecility and sometimes stupidity of a republic like our own, is far better than no government at all. And for this reason, says the Apostle Paul, 'The powers are ordained of God,' not that they are always the best forms of government for the people, or that they afford liberty and freedom to mankind but that any and all forms of government are better than none at all, having a tendency as they do to restrain the passions of human nature and to curb them, and to establish and maintain order to a greater or less degree. One monopoly is better than many; and the oppression of a king is tolerable, but the oppression of a mob, where every man is a law to himself and his own right arm, is his power to enforce his own will, is the worst form of government."

The Book of Mormon's *Art of War* teaches that people are to fight for, not a tyrannical government, but a free one, and leaders like Moroni weren't going to rest until the rights God had intended for a free society to enjoy—that of life, liberty, property, "...our God, our religion, and freedom, and our peace, our wives, and our children." (Alma 26:12), were enjoyed to their fullest.

Other scriptures reaffirming this principle include all of Alma 60, Alma 59:13, and Helaman 1:7-8.

Principle 6 (closely related to Principle 5):

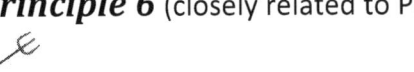

"...whosoever [will] not take up arms in the defence of their country, but [will] fight against it, [are to be] put to death" (Alma 62:9)

In the Book of Mormon, those who would NOT take up arms in defense of their country's freedoms, but who instead would fight against it, committed treason—and were worthy of death. Treason can be defined as "the offense of attempting to overthrow the government of one's country or of assisting its enemies in war." (The New Merriam-Webster Dictionary)

Although in 2012 America, treason against our Constitution seems commonplace, this was not so in the Book of Mormon. Although "the law could have no power on any man for his belief," (Alma 1:17) as soon as actions pertaining to a man's belief caused the death or subjugation of his countrymen, lines of irrepair were crossed. For example:

> And the men of Pachus received their trial, according to the law, and also those king-men who had been taken and cast into prison; and they were executed according to the law; yea, those men of Pachus and those king-men, whosoever would not take up arms in the defence of their country, but would fight against it, *were put to death.*

> And thus it became expedient that this law should be *strictly* observed for the safety of their country; yea, and *whosoever was found denying their freedom* (i.e. the mechanism in place to preserve their freedom, or a Constitution) *was speedily executed according to the law.*
>
> And thus ended the thirtieth year of the reign of the judges over the people of Nephi; Moroni and Pahoran having restored peace to the land of Zarahemla, among their own people, **having inflicted death upon all those who were not true to the cause of freedom**. (Alma 62:9-11)

The Book of Mormon's *king-men* were opposed to the *freemen*, or those who "had sworn or covenanted to maintain their rights and the privileges of their religion by a free government." (Alma 51:6) This is the same oath America's military, politicians, and officers take before being allowed to lawfully perform their duty of office. A counter oath to this would be one in which men swear to rule over others, taking away the freedom, for:

> "...those who were in favor of kings... sought to be kings; and they were supported by those who sought power and authority over the people." (Alma 51:8)

Simply, in the Book of Mormon "whosoever would not take up arms in the defence of their country, but would fight against it [by omission or commission], were put to death" (Alma 62:9) either by execution of the law (Alma 62:9-11), or by arms (Alma 51:17-19).

Sun Tzu would have agreed. He said, "If a secret piece of news is divulged by a spy before the time is ripe, he must be put to death together with the man to whom the secret was told." (Sun Tzu XIII:19)

Sun Bin, a descendent of Sun Tzu and a military strategist who could recite each Principle in Sun Tzu's *Art of War*, himself was framed for treason, and sentenced to death. After a plea, the sentence was changed to face-tattooing and removal of the kneecaps, effectively branding Sun as a criminal and rendering him a handicap for the rest of his life. (www.wikipedia.org/wiki/Sun_Bin)

Other scriptures reaffirming this principle include Alma 46:34-35.

Engaged in War: Interacting with the Enemy

Principle 7:

Love for Your Fellowman is One's Motivation for Going into Battle. Pray for Your Deliverance, but also for your Enemies, Do not Delight in Killing

This principle is two-fold, 1) love your friends and 2) love your enemies. It's much more obvious and easier to love your friends. It's also easier to pray for your friends and fellow comrades in battle, but the act of prayer still needs to be given full attention. In Alma 2:28 we read, "Nevertheless, the Nephites being strengthened by the hand of the Lord, having prayed **mightily** to him that he would deliver them out of the hands of their enemies [in battle], therefore the Lord did hear their cries, and did strengthen them…"

This is a theme throughout the Book of Mormon. As eager as God is to answer your prayers, He cannot, unless and until you actually pray and ask for Him for the desires of your heart.

The harder act is to pray for and love your enemies. Yet this is still needed in order to gain the Lord's approval and strength.

Jesus said:

> And behold it is written also, that thou shalt love thy neighbor and hate thine enemy; But behold I say unto you, love your enemies, bless them that curse you, do good to them that hate you, and pray for them who despitefully use you and persecute you; That ye may be the children of your Father who is in heaven; for he maketh his sun to rise on the evil and on the good. (3 Nephi 12:43-45)

Enos was a Nephite who "saw wars between the Nephites and Lamanites in the course of my days," (Enos 1:24) notwithstanding, his people, the Nephites, "did seek diligently to restore the Lamanites unto the true faith in God." (Enos 1:20) However, it's recorded that:

> ...our labors were vain; their hatred was fixed, and they were led by their evil nature that they became wild, and ferocious, and a blood-thirsty people,

> full of idolatry and filthiness; feeding upon beasts of prey; dwelling in tents, and wandering about in the wilderness with a short skin girdle about their loins and their heads shaven; and their skill was in the bow, and in the cimeter, and the ax. And many of them did eat nothing save it was raw meat; and they were continually seeking to destroy us. (Enos 1:20)
>
> ...And they swore in their wrath that, if it were possible, they would destroy our records and us, and also all the traditions of our fathers. (Enos 1:14)

From a Nephite's perspective, how easy it would have been to hate these people! They were filthy. They were blood-thirsty. They wandered around idly in the wilderness with shaven heads. They were idolaters. *AND* they were constantly seeking to destroy Enos, Nephite traditions, and the sacred records entrusted to him.

Yet Enos had a different attitude. As he was going to hunt beasts in the forest, he remembered his "father speak concerning eternal life, and the joy of the saints, sunk deep into my heart." (Enos 1:3) Dropping to his knees, he prayed to God all the day long. In his prayer, it's recorded that:

> ...I prayed unto him with many long strugglings for my brethren, the Lamanites... And now behold, this was the desire which I desired of him—that if it should so be, that my people, the Nephites, should fall into transgression, and by any means be destroyed, and the Lamanites should not be destroyed, that the Lord God would preserve a record of my people, the Nephites; even if it so be by the power of his holy arm, that it might be brought forth at some future day unto the Lamanites, that, perhaps, they might be brought unto salvation. (Enos 1:11,13)

This kind of love gains the approval of the Lord. "For if ye love them which love you [only], what reward have ye? do not even the publicans the same?" (Matthew 5:46)

Because of Enos' great love and faith, finally the Lord said unto him:

> ...I will grant unto thee according to thy desires, because of thy faith. (Enos 1:12)

Perhaps the oddest of feelings, during battle the Lord requires love for the people you are killing—even while in the act of killing them. Moroni's army had this love, for it's recorded that:

> Now, they were sorry to take up arms against the Lamanites, because they did not delight in the shedding of blood; yea, and this was not all—they were sorry to be the means of sending so many of their brethren out of this world into an eternal world, unprepared to meet their God. Nevertheless, they could not suffer to lay down their lives, that their wives and their children should be massacred by the barbarous cruelty... (Alma 48:23-24)

Other scriptures reaffirming this principle include all of Mormon 7, Alma 44:1-2, Alma 48:16, Alma 55:19.

Principle 8:

Your Leaders Must be Mighty Men of Humility, Faith, and Prayer (who make it Perfectly Clear within the Ranks as to the Cause for Which they are Fighting)

In the Book of Mormon, the cause for which righteous armies engage in war is crystal clear, since war is always defensive. Soldiers are fighting for their land, their wives and children, their peace, their freedom, and their religion. (Alma 46:12) Because of this, righteous soldiers are well aware that their enemy's banner in war is nothing less than a desire to seek power and authority. (Alma 60:17) This theme is reiterated throughout the entire Book of Mormon's recording of wars. For example Moroni, in Alma 60, closes an epistle with these words:

> Behold, I am Moroni, your chief captain. I seek not for power, but to pull it down. I seek not for honor of the world, but for the glory of my God, and the freedom and welfare of my country. (Alma 60:36)

However, Ammoron, a Lamanite leader and power-seeker, closes his epistle to Moroni with:

> And behold now, I am a bold Lamanite; behold, this war hath been waged to avenge their wrongs, and to maintain and to obtain their rights to the government; (Alma 54:24)

When Moroni received Ammoron's epistle, he was angered:

> ...because he knew that Ammoron had a perfect knowledge of his fraud; yea, he knew that Ammoron knew that it was not a just cause that had caused him to wage a war against the people of Nephi. (Alma 55:1)

Likewise, the Gadianton power-seeker Giddianhi sent an epistle to Lachoneus asking him to turn over all the lands and possessions of the Nephites. As justification for the power grab, Giddianhi writes:

> And I write this epistle unto you, Lachoneus, and I hope that ye will deliver up your lands and your possessions... that this my people may recover their rights and government, who have dissented away from you because of your wickedness in retaining from them their rights of

> government, and except ye do this, I
> will avenge their wrongs. (3 Nephi 3:10)

Like Moroni, Lachoneus' reaction was one of anger, yet also perplex. It's recorded that Lachoneus was:

> ...exceedingly astonished, because of the boldness of Giddianhi demanding the possession of the land of the Nephites, and also of threatening the people and avenging the wrongs of those that had received no wrong, save it were they had wronged themselves by dissenting away unto those wicked and abominable robbers. Now behold, this Lachoneus, the governor, was a just man, and could not be frightened by the demands and the threatenings of a robber; (3 Nephi 3:11-12)

And herein is the power that builds confidence in soldiers—knowing that their cause is just, and that righteous leaders are spearheading efforts for a just and godly rebellion. In the case of Lachoneus' efforts to battle the Gadianton robbers who were seeking power, it's recorded that:

> Lachoneus did appoint chief captains over all the armies of the Nephites...

> Now the chiefest among all the chief captains and the great commander of all the armies of the Nephites was appointed, and his name was Gidgiddoni. Now it was the custom among all the Nephites to appoint for their chief captains, (save it were in their times of wickedness) some one that had the spirit of revelation and also prophecy; therefore, **this Gidgiddoni was a great prophet among them, as also was the chief judge** [**Lachoneus himself**]. (3 Nephi 3:18-19)

Certainly it was the custom of the righteous armies in the Book of Mormon to appoint mighty men of God to lead military efforts. As one additional example, Jarom records:

> And it came to pass that they [the Lamanites] came many times against us, the Nephites, to battle. But... our leaders were mighty men in the faith of the Lord; and they taught the people the ways of the Lord; wherefore, we withstood the Lamanites and swept them away out of our lands... (Jarom 1:7)

Contrast this principle with those principles that currently control America's armed forces, where fighting seems never to be in defense of U.S. soil, but preemptive on other nation's land; with soldiers NOT fighting for their wives and children, their religion and their God, but to feed into conspiring men's plans for economic collapse and world slavery.

This Book of Mormon's *Art of War* Principle 8 is the eternal echo of the Lord's words to Samuel:

> ...for them that honour me I will honour, and they that despise me shall be lightly esteemed. (1 Samuel 2:30)

Other scriptures reaffirming this principle include Alma 2:29-31, Alma 26:22, Alma 46:11-13, Alma 46:19-22, Alma 48:13, Alma 53:2, Alma 56:44-47, Alma 58:10-11, Alma 58:40, Alma 62:4-5, Alma 62:40-41, 51, All of 3 Nephi 3, 3 Nephi 6:6.

Principle 9:

Use Strategy, which involves Deceit ("Attack him where he is unprepared, appear where you are not expected" from Sun Tzu)

Sun Tzu says "All warfare is based on Deception" (Sun Tzu I:18) and "Attack him where he is unprepared, appear where you are not expected." (Sun Tzu I:24)

The Book of Mormon is filled with stories of righteous leaders drawing out the enemy under false pretenses (Alma 52:16-40), attacking when the enemy is unprepared (Alma 43:15-54), and appearing where not expected (Alma 55:4-25).

What's important, however, is to realize that this is a principle that a wicked enemy has access to as well (Alma 51:22-26, Mormon 4:2, Helaman 1:9-12) Principle 9 is a reinforcement of Sun Tzu's detailed principles, and a testimony to his genius.

Other scriptures reaffirming this principle include Alma 49:4-5, Alma 50:12, Alma 62:20-22, Helaman 2:6-9.

Principle 10:

The Most Effective Means of Defense is to Fortify Areas of Possible Invasion

Since it is the purpose of all godly armies to fight in defense, and never in offense, this principle holds special significance. In a popular board game of world conquest, the strategist who "attacks" his opponent rolls 3 dice, while the defender rolls 2 dice. The advantage to the defender is that if there is a tie in the value of each competitor's die, the defender wins. Statistically this computes to the defender winning 58.33% of the time, and the attacker winning 41.67% of the time—advantage defender! This advantage to the defender holds true in real war as well, with the odds likely being much higher, according to win/loss percentages in the Book of Mormon:

> And now as Moroni had supposed that there should be men sent to the city of Nephihah, to the assistance of the people to maintain that city, and knowing that it was *easier to keep the city from falling into the hands of the Lamanites than to retake it from them*, he supposed that they would easily maintain that city. (Alma 59:9)

In the story of Lachoneus preparing for war against the Gadianton robbers, it's recorded that:

> Yea, he sent a proclamation among all the people, that they should gather together their women, and their children, their flocks and their herds,

> and all their substance, save it were their land, unto one place. And he caused that fortifications should be built round about them, and the strength thereof should be exceedingly great. And he caused that armies, both of the Nephites and of the Lamanites, or of all them who were numbered among the Nephites, should be placed as guards round about to watch them, and to guard them from the robbers day and night. (3 Nephi 3:13-14)

The result was success, since:

> Therefore, there was no chance for the robbers to plunder and to obtain food, save it were to come up in open battle against the Nephites; and the Nephites being in one body, and having so great a number, and having reserved for themselves provisions, and horses and cattle, and flocks of every kind, that they might subsist for the space of seven years, in the which time they did hope to destroy the robbers from off the face of the land; (3 Nephi 4:4)

Moroni practiced principle 10 in defending his people against king Amalickiah's armies—to the great astonishment and disappointment of the Lamanite leaders at Ammonihah:

> And behold, the city had been rebuilt, and Moroni had stationed an army by the borders of the city, and they had cast up dirt round about to shield them from the arrows and the stones of the Lamanites... [and] how great was their disappointment; for behold, the Nephites had dug up a ridge of earth round about them, which was so high that the Lamanites could not cast their stones and their arrows at them that they might take effect... [and] the chief captains of the Lamanites were astonished exceedingly, because of the wisdom of the Nephites in preparing their places of security. (Alma 49:2-5)

The result of this tactic was success:

> Now when they found that they could not obtain power over the Nephites by the pass, they began to dig down their banks of earth that they might obtain a pass to their armies, that they might

have an equal chance to fight; but behold, in these attempts they were swept off by the stones and arrows which were thrown at them; and instead of filling up their ditches by pulling down the banks of earth, they were filled up in a measure with their dead and wounded bodies. Thus the Nephites had all power over their enemies; and thus the Lamanites did attempt to destroy the Nephites until their chief captains were all slain; yea, and more than a thousand of the Lamanites were slain; while, on the other hand, there was not a single soul of the Nephites which was slain. (Alma 49:22-23)

An important element of this principle is not only the preparation of infrastructure, but provisions for those "locked" inside, such as food, water, and medical supplies. Should your enemy lay siege, as happened in 3rd Nephi 4, if preparations are made beforehand, success will be likely, as it was with the Nephites. For it's recorded that:

> But behold, this was an advantage to the Nephites; for it was impossible for the robbers to lay siege sufficiently long

to have any effect upon the Nephites,
because of their much provision which
they had laid up in store, (3 Nephi 4:18)

Other scriptures reaffirming this principle include Alma 49:4-5, Alma 49:13-15, Alma 52:9, Alma 53:3-6, 3 Nephi 3:25, 3 Nephi 4:16-19.

Principle 11:

Confronting a Potential Enemy's Intent may be Necessary, with Good Judgment, to Ascertain their Plans

There are three occasions in the Book of Mormon when developing events, if left unchecked, would have resulted in substantial long-term consequences, "which consequences would lead to the overthrow of their liberty." (Alma 50:32) Two of these are attributable to dissensions among the Nephites. In such cases the Book of Mormon shows us that a wise commander will, with his army, confront the would-be traitors in an act of non-aggression to substantiate their intent.

When Amalickiah stirred up a portion of the people, who had called themselves Amalickiahites, Moroni began assembling his army to "gather together all the people who were desirous to maintain their liberty, to stand against Amalickiah and those who had dissented." (Alma 46:28) When Moroni started to become successful, Amalickiah, fearing he would lose power among a people who were beginning to doubt their cause (Alma 46:29), took those who would go with him and departed out of the land with the intent to join with the Lamanites. Then the record states:

> Now Moroni thought it was not expedient that the Lamanites should have any more strength; therefore he thought to cut off the people of Amalickiah, or to take them and bring them back, and put Amalickiah to death [for treason, see Principle 6]; yea, for he knew that he would stir up the Lamanites to anger against them [like he did the Nephites], and cause them to come to battle against them; and this he knew that Amalickiah would do that he might obtain his purposes.
>
> Therefore Moroni thought it was expedient that he should take his armies, who had gathered themselves together, and armed themselves, and

entered into a covenant to keep the peace—and it came to pass that he took his army and marched out with his tents into the wilderness, to cut off the course of Amalickiah in the wilderness.

And it came to pass that he did according to his desires, and marched forth into the wilderness, and headed the armies of Amalickiah. And it came to pass that Amalickiah fled with a small number of his men, and the remainder were delivered up into the hands of Moroni and were taken back into the land of Zarahemla... And it came to pass that whomsoever of the Amalickiahites that would not enter into a covenant to support the cause of freedom, that they might maintain a free government, he caused to be put to death... (Alma 46:30-35)

A similar story (also involving Moroni) took place as recorded in Alma 50:25-36; and the third, involving Gidgiddoni, is recorded in 3 Nephi 4:23-27 as he ordered his armies to cut off the Gadianton army's retreat.

In all three cases there was opportunity for the enemy's peaceful surrender, entrance into a covenant to support the cause of freedom, and their final liberation. (in the case of Gidgiddoni, see 3 Nephi 5:4).

Principle 12:

Make Use of Spies

Although the Book of Mormon doesn't go into great depth on categories of spies, as does Sun Tzu (see Sun Tzu's *Art of War* XIII, "The Use of Spies"), it is evident that righteous armies use the services of spies.

The scriptures tell us that:

> And Moroni placed spies round about, that he might know when the camp of the Lamanites should come. (Alma 43:28)

Other scriptures reaffirming this principle include Alma 2:21, Alma 43:23, Alma 43:30, Alma 50: 30-31, Alma 56:22, Alma 57:30, Alma 62:20.

Principle 13:

Utilize Those Men of God With The Spirit of Prophecy, and are able to "inquire of the Lord" as to Specific war Strategies

In addition to spies, Moroni and other righteous army leaders made use of those with the spirit of prophecy:

> But it came to pass, as soon as they had departed into the wilderness Moroni sent spies into the wilderness to watch their camp; and Moroni, also, knowing of the prophecies of Alma, sent certain men unto him, desiring him that he should inquire of the Lord whither the armies of the Nephites should go to defend themselves against the Lamanites.
>
> And it came to pass that the word of the Lord came unto Alma, and Alma informed the messengers of Moroni... And those messengers went and delivered the message unto Moroni. (Alma 43:23-24)

Zoram utilized the spirit of prophecy, as well, to recover all of the prisoners of war that the Lamanites had taken. Alma's instructions from the Lord to Zoram are rather specific:

> Zoram..., knowing that Alma was high priest over the church, and having heard that he had the spirit of prophecy, therefore they went unto him and desired of him to know whither the Lord would that they should go into the wilderness in search of their brethren, who had been taken captive by the Lamanites.
>
> And it came to pass that Alma inquired of the Lord concerning the matter. And Alma returned and said unto them: Behold, the Lamanites will cross the river Sidon in the south wilderness, away up beyond the borders of the land of Manti. And behold there shall ye meet them, on the east of the river Sidon, and there the Lord will deliver unto thee thy brethren who have been taken captive by the Lamanites... And [so] they came upon the armies of the Lamanites, and the Lamanites were scattered and driven into the wilderness; and they took their brethren who had been taken captive

by the Lamanites, and there was not one soul of them had been lost that were taken captive. (Alma 16:5-8)

Battling an enemy "in the strength of the Lord" means tapping into this powerful principle, a principle perhaps not utilized for many hundreds of years.

The promise in the Book of Mormon was that:

> ...if they were faithful in keeping the commandments of God... he would prosper them in the land; yea, warn them to flee, or to prepare for war, according to their danger; And also, that God would make it known unto them whither they should go to defend themselves against their enemies, and by so doing, the Lord would deliver them... (Alma 48:15-16)

Other scriptures reaffirming this principle include Mosiah 24:23, Alma 56:30-47, Alma 57:8-12, Alma 58:15-27.

Principle 14:

Prepare Adequate Weapons for War

Although this would seem obvious, many a war has been won or lost because of adequate, and/or inadequate, preparations of weapons.

Jarom tells us:

> And we multiplied exceedingly... and became exceedingly rich in gold, and in silver, and in precious things... making all manner of tools of every kind to till the ground, and weapons of war—yea, the sharp pointed arrow, and the quiver, and the dart, and the javelin, and all preparations for war. And thus being prepared to meet the Lamanites, they did not prosper against us. But the word of the Lord was verified, which he spake unto our fathers, saying that: Inasmuch as ye will keep my commandments ye shall prosper in the land. (Jarom 1:8-9)

In his 5th annual address to Congress on Dec 13, 1793, George Washington made this remark:

> "If we desire to avoid insult, we must be able to repel it; if we desire to secure peace, one of the most powerful instruments of our rising prosperity, it must be known that we are at all times ready for war."

Other scriptures reaffirming this principle include Mosiah 10:1, Alma 43:19-21, Alma 43:37-38, Alma 48:7-11, Alma 49:22, Alma 51:31, Alma 52:19, Alma 53:7, 3 Nephi 3:26, Ether 10:27.

Principle 15:

During Actual Battle, Put your Trust in the Strength of the Lord, and have Courage, because of your Cause

It's recorded that the people of Nephi, "as they were crossing the river Sidon, the Lamanites and the Amlicites, being as numerous almost, as it were, as the sands of the sea, came upon them to destroy them." (Alma 2:27)

> Nevertheless, the Nephites being *strengthened by the hand of the Lord*, having prayed mightily to him that he

> would deliver them out of the hands of their enemies, therefore the Lord did hear their cries, and did strengthen them, and the Lamanites and the Amlicites did fall before them.
>
> And it came to pass that Alma fought with Amlici with the sword, face to face; and they did contend mightily, one with another. And it came to pass that Alma, being a man of God, being exercised with much faith, cried, saying: O Lord, have mercy and spare my life, that I may be an instrument in thy hands to save and preserve this people. Now when Alma had said these words he contended again with Amlici; and he was strengthened, insomuch that he slew Amlici with the sword. (see Alma 2:28-31)

Faith and prayers can and should occur *before* battle, but also *during* battle. The Lord said his disciples "should not cease to pray in their hearts." (3 Nephi 20:1) The horrors of battle truly separate godly men who believe in the cause of freedom, from godless men whose purpose is only to kill and enslave.

Joseph Reed, who was an adjutant general to George Washington, and a close confidant, said of the men fighting in 1776:

> "When I look around and see how few of the numbers who talked to loudly of death and honor are around me, I am lost in wonder and surprise. Your noisy *sons of liberty* are, I find, the quietest on the field... An engagement, or even the expectation of one, gives a wonderful insight into character." (*Life and Correspondence of Joseph Reed*, by William Bradford Reed, p. 241)

When one calls upon God in faith, one takes upon himself God's strength, which nothing can defeat. Whatever then happens will be in line with His holy and all-knowing purposes. Alma wanted to be preserved that he might be an instrument in the hands of the Lord to "save and preserve this people." God knew Alma's motives to be pure. Alma may not have been as skilled with the sword as Amlici, but God is much more skilled—a strength He gave unto Alma upon request. (see Alma 2:29-31) Purity of heart trumps secular skill—just as the heavens are higher than the earth.

Wherefore, I call upon the weak things of the world, those who are unlearned and despised, to thresh the nations by the power of my Spirit; And their arm shall be my arm, and I will be their shield and their buckler; and I will gird up their loins, and they shall fight manfully for me; and their enemies shall be under their feet; and I will let fall the sword in their behalf, and by the fire of mine indignation will I preserve them. (Doctrine & Covenants 35:13-14)

Other scriptures reaffirming this principle include Mosiah 10:10, Mosiah 10:19, Alma 2:27-28, Mosiah 20:11, Alma 56:44-47, Alma 57:21, 3 Nephi 4:9-10.

Principle 16:

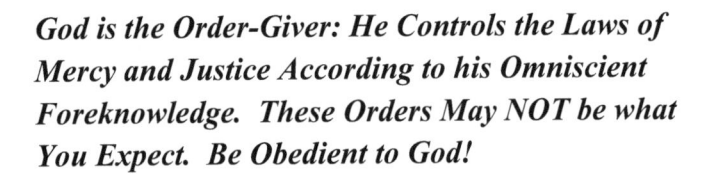

God is the Order-Giver: He Controls the Laws of Mercy and Justice According to his Omniscient Foreknowledge. These Orders May NOT be what You Expect. Be Obedient to God!

This is a principle that requires a familiarity with the Spirit, and a maturity of soul. Critics of this principle would say that most of the godless wars that have been fought in all of history have been (and will be) fought because "God told somebody to do something." Indeed Satan, that great deceiver, takes the godly principle of revelation, and substitutes an illusion in its place with the ever-destroying theme of 'the end justifies the means.' Those who are not worthy, or are only partially worthy will easily be deceived.

John the Revelator tells us, "And the great dragon... deceiveth the whole world..." (Revelations 12:9)

We live in an age of deceit. "O my people," said Isaiah in the Book of Mormon, "they who lead thee cause thee to err and destroy the way of thy paths." (2 Nephi 13:12)

"Even within the Church" says Ezra Taft Benson, "we have been warned that 'the ravening wolves are amongst us, from our own membership, and they, more than any others, are clothed in sheep's clothing, because they wear the habiliments of the priesthood.'" (Ezra Taft Benson quotes J. Reuben Clark, Jr., Conference Report, April 1949, p. 163., *Civic Standards for the Saints*, 1972)

The Holy Spirit can only be discerned by one who lives righteously—one who accepts and keeps sacred covenants, then strives to foster an intimate personal relationship with our Father in Heaven. Despite the doubters and naysayers, men have been inspired through the ages.

> And I looked and beheld a man among the Gentiles, who was separated from the seed of my brethren by the many waters; and I beheld the Spirit of God, that it came down and wrought upon the man; and he went forth upon the many waters, even unto the seed of my brethren, who were in the promised land. (1 Nephi 13:12)

The Lord had control of the discovery and the colonization of America. Nephi was told that there was a man among the gentiles who was "wrought upon" by the Spirit of God, and under that inspiration he came to America. Here is what Columbus himself said about being guided from on high:

> I have seen, and truly I have studied all books and cosmographies, histories, chronicles, and philosophies and other arts for which our Lord with provident hand unlocked my mind, sent me upon the seas and gave me fire for the deed. Those who heard of my enterprise called it foolish, mocked me, and laughed, but who can doubt but that

> the Holy Ghost inspired me? (Jacob Wasserman, Columbus, *Don Quixote of the Seas*, p. 18)

When Columbus went to King Ferdinand, he said, "I came to Your Majesty as the emissary of the Holy Ghost." When he stood before the clergy of San Esteban, he insisted to them that he must be regarded as a man inspired. (As quoted in *"The Great Prologue"*, by Elder Mark E. Petersen, a fireside address given at Brigham Young University on September 29, 1974)

Indeed, men and women have been inspired by God throughout the ages; and with this inspiration, have *even instigated offensive war*, with the only difference in right or wrong being that God, through revelation, did or did not instruct his servants to venture. Joseph Smith said:

> "God said, 'Thou shalt not kill;' at another time He said, 'Thou shalt utterly destroy.' This is the principle on which the government of heaven is conducted—*by revelation* adapted to the circumstances in which the children of the kingdom are placed. Whatever God requires is right no matter what it is, although we may not see the reason

> thereof..." (Teachings of the Prophet Joseph Smith, p. 256)

The Church's online manual for the Old Testament elaborates on the story of when Abraham deceived the Pharaoh by telling him that his wife was his sister. The manual gives this final summation:

> "...he did deceive the Egyptians. How can this action be justified? The answer is very simple. His action was justified because God told him to do it (see Abraham 2:22–25)." (see www.institute.lds.org/courses/ for this scripture)

Consider in the Book of Mormon the story of the Anti-Nephi-Lehites, who made a covenant with God that they would never again lift up a sword, even in *defending* their own lives. King Lamoni stated to his people:

> Now, my best beloved brethren, since God hath taken away our stains, and our swords have become bright, then let us stain our swords no more with the blood of our brethren. Behold, I say unto you, Nay, let us retain our swords that they be not stained with

> the blood of our brethren; for perhaps, if we should stain our swords again they can no more be washed bright through the blood of the Son of our great God, which shall be shed for the atonement of our sins. (Alma 24:12-13)

Yet an entirely different commandment was given to another group of people, although close-knit with King Lamoni's Anti-Nephi-Lehites:

> ...the Lord had said unto them, and also unto their fathers, that: Inasmuch as ye are not guilty of the first offense, neither the second, ye shall not suffer yourselves to be slain by the hands of your enemies. And again, the Lord has said that: Ye shall defend your families even unto bloodshed. (Alma 43:46-47)

Nephi was told to kill Laban, even though Nephi said in his heart, "Never at any time have I shed the blood of man. And I shrunk and would that I might not slay him." (1 Nephi 4:10) Yet he "did obey the voice of the Spirit, and took Laban by the hair of the head, and smote off his head with his own sword." (1 Nephi 4:18)

Deviating from the rule of allowing a captured soldier the option of undertaking a covenant of peace and being set at liberty (see principle 23), Gidgiddoni, a great prophet (see 3 Nephi 3:19) chose instead to "not spare any that should fall into their hands":

> And it came to pass that Gidgiddoni commanded that his armies should pursue them as far as the borders of the wilderness, and that they should not spare any that should fall into their hands by the way; and thus they did pursue them and did slay them, to the borders of the wilderness, even until they had fulfilled the commandment of Gidgiddoni. (3 Nephi 4:13)

Granted, Gidgiddoni may have determined that these Gadianton robbers were all guilty of treason, and thus deserved to die (see Principle 6), yet Gidgiddoni allowed other Gadianton robbers the opportunity to repent, be liberated (3 Nephi 5:4), and eventually "granted [them]... lands, according to their numbers, that they might have, with their labors, wherewith to subsist upon..." (3 Nephi 6:3)

When it comes to obeying this Book of Mormon *Art of War* Principle, it's paramount to follow the old adage, "Those who know, rather than those *who think they know*, should be the ones who are in charge." May God bless all with the righteous, Holy Ghost inspired, discernment and testimony of those whom He calls upon to lead soldiers. (see principle 7)

Other scriptures reaffirming this principle include Alma 20:24, Alma 55:3, 3 Nephi 3:15, 3 Nephi 4:13, Ezekiel 9, Joshua 6:21, Deuteronomy 7:1-2, Deuteronomy 20:16-18.

Principle 17:

Don't Fear Death, Value your Liberty More than your Life

One of the greatest stories in the Book of Mormon is the miraculous display of courage shown by the 2,000, and then later 2,060 stripling warriors who were the sons of the Anti-Nephi-Lehites. These youth were "firm and undaunted" and did "obey and observe to perform every word of command with exactness." (Alma 57:20-21)

In a major battle with the Lamanites, these warriors joined the Nephites in defending their cause. After the ordeal was over the record states:

> ...according to the goodness of God, and to our great astonishment, and also the joy of our whole army, there was not one soul of them who did perish; yea, and neither was there one soul among them who had not received many wounds. And now, their preservation was astonishing to our whole army, yea, that they should be spared while there was a thousand of our brethren who were slain. And we do justly ascribe it to the miraculous power of God, because of their exceeding faith in that which they had been taught to believe—that there was a just God, and whosoever did not doubt, that they should be preserved by his marvelous power. (Alma 57:25-26)

But there was an additional secret to their success. The record states:

> Now they never had fought, yet they did not fear death; and *they did think more upon the liberty of their fathers than they did upon their lives...* (Alma 56:47)

The phrase "of their fathers" appears forty-one times in the Book of Mormon. There are several words that appear *before* this phrase, such as *iniquities* (5 times), and *land* (2 times), but by far the most predominant word is *traditions*, appearing in over half (21 times) of the forty-one occurrences. Thus another way to read this scripture would be:

> Now they never had fought, yet they did not fear death; and they did think more upon the liberty <u>that was the traditions</u> of their fathers than they did upon their lives...

The Founding Fathers of America considered there to be three great and equal causes for which they were to fight. These were *life*, *liberty* and *property*. Cleon Skousen teaches the principle that these three are co-equal, in his book "The 5,000 Year Leap." (Principle 15)

Declaration of Independence signer, Samuel Adams, stood in front of the *then* 29 members of Continental Congress in York, Pennsylvania, at a time when there seemed to be little hope for the Revolution's success, and stated:

> "We have proclaimed to the world our determination to die freemen, rather

than to live slaves. We have appealed to heaven for the justice of our cause, and in heaven we have placed our trust." (Samuel Adams: A Life, by Ira Stoll, p. 4)

On the value of property, John Adams said:

"The moment the idea is admitted into society that property is not as sacred as the laws of God, and that there is not a force of law and public justice to protect it, anarchy and tyranny commence. *Property must be secured, or liberty cannot exist.*" (John Adams, The Works of John Adams, 6:9, p. 280)

Finally Ezra Taft Benson said, unequivocally, that:

"Freedom is a God-given eternal principle, a heritage more precious than life itself." ("Ezra Taft Benson of the Council of the Twelve," Improvement Era, November 1966)

One of the great examples in all of holy writ is contained in the story of the 2,060 stripling warriors, because of their approach to war. Each valued his liberty more than his life, which gave the collection of these young men power from on high to go forward *in the strength of the Lord.*

Other scriptures reaffirming this principle include Alma 56:11, Alma 60:13, Alma 27:28-29.

Principle 18:

To Kill the Leader of an Enemy's Army Privily is to Gain Great Advantage

In war, all men are not equal in their abilities, both in the skill of war, and in stirring up their countrymen to a cause. Captain Moroni was successful in stirring up his countrymen to fight for the cause of their liberty, land, wives, children, and their rights of worship (see Alma 46). Yet likewise Amalickiah, who had dissented from the Nephites, was masterful in the craft of stirring up people to unrighteous anger—much like men today use the media and unsound philosophy to stir up the American people towards angrily supporting an unjust cause such as unconstitutional wars.

The scriptures tell us:

> ...Amalickiah... had taken those who went with him, and went up in the land of Nephi among the Lamanites, and did stir up the Lamanites to anger against the people of Nephi, insomuch that the king of the Lamanites sent a proclamation throughout all his land, among all his people, that they should gather themselves together again to go to battle against the Nephites. (Alma 47:1)

Then again, later:

> ...for behold, Amalickiah had again stirred up the hearts of the people of the Lamanites against the people of the Nephites, and he was gathering together soldiers from all parts of his land, and arming them, and preparing for war with all diligence; for he had sworn to drink the blood of Moroni. (Alma 51:9)

No wonder there is a pause in the record in which is stated, concerning Amalickiah:

> Thus we see how... the great wickedness one very wicked man can

> cause to take place among the children of men. Yea, we see that Amalickiah, because he was a man of cunning device and a man of many flattering words, that he led away the hearts of many people to do wickedly; yea, and to seek to destroy the church of God, and to destroy the foundation of liberty which God had granted unto them, or which blessing God had sent upon the face of the land for the righteous' sake. (Alma 46:8-10)

To have caught and put to death Amalickiah early on (Moroni's original intention), would have saved innumerable lives and many years of grief. Hence, Amalickiah's death, along with other high-profile officers, would have provided (and did provide later) a much weightier victory than the common rank-in-file subordinate.

Moroni's friend in liberty, Teancum, knew this, which is why he crept into the camp of the Lamanites one night. It's recorded that:

> ...Teancum and his servant stole forth and went out by night, and went into the camp of Amalickiah; and behold, sleep had overpowered them because

of their much fatigue, which was caused by the labors and heat of the day. And it came to pass that Teancum stole privily into the tent of the king, and put a javelin to his heart; and he did cause the death of the king immediately that he did not awake his servants. (Alma 51:33-34)

With the aid of spies, and through strategy, pivotal leaders can be found and destroyed before their plots come to fruition. The last of Sun Tzu's principles of "Waging War" says, "Thus it may be known that the leader of armies is the arbiter of the people's fate, the man on whom it depends whether the nation shall be in peace or in peril." (Sun Tzu's *Art of War*, II:20)

Other scriptures reaffirming this principle include Alma 62:36, Ether 7:18.

Principle 19:

During Pivotal Moments, the Leader Must Inspire His Soldiers with Memorable and Inspirational Remarks

One of the segments in the movie "Braveheart" that is played over and over again in various media circles records William Wallace's passionate and patriotic plea to the doubting Scottish band timidly pursuing Independence. It carries the following line:

> "I *am* William Wallace; and I see a whole army of my countrymen, here in defiance of tyranny! You have come to fight as free men. And free man you are! What will you do without freedom? Will you fight?"
>
> "Against that?"– a veteran shouted. "No! We will run, and we will live!"
>
> "Yes!" Wallace shouted back. "Fight and you may die. Run and you will live, at least awhile. And dying in your beds many years from now, would you be willing to trade all the days from this day to that for one chance, just one chance, to come back here and tell our enemies that they may take our lives but they will never take our freedom!"

Captain Moroni was the "William Wallace" of the Book of Mormon, for it's recorded that:

> ...when the men of Moroni saw the fierceness and the anger of the Lamanites, they were about to shrink and flee from them. And Moroni, perceiving their intent, sent forth and inspired their hearts with these thoughts—yea, the thoughts of their lands, their liberty, yea, their freedom from bondage. And it came to pass that they turned upon the Lamanites, and they cried with one voice unto the Lord their God, for their liberty and their freedom from bondage. And they began to stand against the Lamanites with power; and in that selfsame hour that they cried unto the Lord for their freedom, the Lamanites began to flee before them; and they fled even to the waters of Sidon. (Alma 43:48-50)

Inspiring words of leaders while in the midst of battle are precious moments that live in infamy for the ranks of soldiers thus led. Leader's remarks are reservoirs of spiritual strength, and should be boldly and passionately expressed.

Specific remarks from the Book of Mormon include:

> (From one of Moroni's guards) *Even as this scalp has fallen to the earth, which is the scalp of your chief, so shall ye fall to the earth except ye will deliver up your weapons of war and depart with a covenant of peace.* (Alma 44:14)

And:

> (from Moroni himself) *Behold, whosoever will maintain this title upon the land, let them come forth in the strength of the Lord, and enter into a covenant that they will maintain their rights, and their religion, that the Lord God may bless them.* (Alma 46:20)

Two-time Pulitzer winning author David McCullough gave an address on the campus of BYU in 2006 where he told a story of how George Washington used Principle 19 to arouse the indispensible support of doubting troops, fighting for America's independence. Says he:

> "In conclusion I want to share a scene that took place on the last day of the year of 1776, December 31st. All the enlistments for the entire army were up. Every soldier, because of the

system at the time, was free to go home as of the first day of January 1777. Washington called a large part of the troops out into formation. He appeared in front of these ragged men on his horse, and he urged them to reenlist. He said that if they would sign up for another six months, he'd give them a bonus of 10 dollars. It was an enormous amount then because that's about what they were being paid for a month—if and when they could get paid. These were men who were desperate for pay of any kind. Their families were starving.

"The drums rolled, and he asked those who would stay on to step forward. The drums kept rolling, and nobody stepped forward. Washington turned and rode away from them. Then he stopped, and he turned back and rode up to them again. And this is what we know he said:

"My brave fellows, you have done all I asked you to do, and more than could be reasonably expected, but your country is at stake, your wives, your

houses, and all that you hold dear. You have worn yourselves out with fatigues and hardships, but we know not how to spare you. If you will consent to stay one month longer, you will render that service to the cause of liberty, and to your country, which you can probably never do under any other circumstance.

"Again the drums rolled. This time the men began stepping forward. "God Almighty," wrote Nathanael Greene, "inclined their hearts to listen to the proposal and they engaged anew."

"Now that is an amazing scene, to say the least, and it's real! This wasn't some contrivance of a screenwriter. However, I believe there is something very familiar about what Washington said to those troops. It was as if he was saying, "You are fortunate. You have a chance to serve your country in a way that nobody else is going to be able to, and everybody else is going to be jealous of you, and you will count this the most important decision and the most valuable service of your lives."

("The Glorious Cause of America," BYU Magazine, Winter 2006)

Other scriptures reaffirming this principle include 3 Nephi 3:15-16, 3 Nephi 4:28-33 (3 specific cries, all different).

Principle 20:

Respect the Rights and Freedoms on Others to NOT engage in Bloodshed, Who have made a Covenant of Peace

War is victory to Satan. He is the author of misery, and it's to his ultimate purpose to cause and promote death. In war, no matter which side wins, Satan's purposes are accomplished. As always, Jesus' words are the solution to Satan's conspiracies and counterfeits. Christ teaches to fight evil with good. "…ye shall *not* resist evil," He says, "but whosoever shall smite thee on thy right cheek, turn to him the other also." (3 Nephi 12:39) He also teaches, "love your enemies, bless them that curse you, do good to them that hate you, and pray for them who despitefully use you and persecute you;" (3 Nephi 12:44)

Likewise Paul says, "Recompense to no man evil for evil." (Romans 12:17)

In the Book of Mormon we read of a people who put their trust in God so completely, that rather than risk committing sin, they:

> ...prostrated themselves... to the earth, and began to call on the name of the Lord; and thus they were in this attitude when the Lamanites began to fall upon them, and began to slay them with the sword. And thus without meeting any resistance, [the Lamanites] did slay a thousand and five of them... (Alma 24:21-22)

These were the people of the Anti-Nephi-Lehites, paying the ultimate sacrifice for their religion. For their king, Lamoni, had told them:

> Now, my best beloved brethren, since God hath taken away our stains, and our swords have become bright, then let us stain our swords no more with the blood of our brethren. Behold, I say unto you, Nay, let us retain our swords that they be not stained with the blood of our brethren; for perhaps,

> if we should stain our swords again they can no more be washed bright through the blood of the Son of our great God, which shall be shed for the atonement of our sins. (Alma 24:12-13)

As it turns out, in the story of this battle:

> ...when the Lamanites saw [their brethren prostrated to the earth] they did forbear from slaying them; and there were many whose hearts had swollen in them for those of their brethren who had fallen under the sword, for they repented of the things which they had done. And it came to pass that they threw down their weapons of war, and they would not take them again, for they were stung for the murders which they had committed; and they came down even as their brethren, relying upon the mercies of those whose arms were lifted to slay them.
>
> And it came to pass that the people of God were joined that day by more than the number who had been slain... (Alma 24:24-26)

Later in the Book of Mormon the Anti-Nephi-Lehites became known as the people of Ammon (or Ammonites), and a more flattering description of them could not be written as in Alma 27; for they were:

> ...distinguished for their zeal towards God, and also towards men; for they were perfectly honest and upright in all things; and they were firm in the faith of Christ, even unto the end. And they did look upon shedding the blood of their brethren with the greatest abhorrence; and they never could be prevailed upon to take up arms against their brethren; and they never did look upon death with any degree of terror, for their hope and views of Christ and the resurrection; therefore, death was swallowed up to them by the victory of Christ over it. Therefore, they would suffer death in the most aggravating and distressing manner which could be inflicted by their brethren, before they would take the sword or cimeter to smite them.

> And thus they were a zealous and beloved people, a highly favored people of the Lord. (Alma 27:27-30)

Yet even as Christ taught "resist *not* evil" (Matthew 5:39), the great patriot Pahoran's advice, shared by Captain Moroni, was for their armies to "resist evil" (Alma 61:14):

> ...let us resist evil, and whatsoever evil we cannot resist with our words, yea, such as rebellions and dissensions, let us resist them with our swords, that we may retain our freedom, that we may rejoice in the great privilege of our church, and in the cause of our Redeemer and our God. (Alma 61:14)

As well:

> ...for the Lord had said unto them, and also unto their fathers, that: Inasmuch as ye are not guilty of the first offense, neither the second, ye shall not suffer yourselves to be slain by the hands of your enemies. And again, the Lord has said that: Ye shall defend your families even unto bloodshed. Therefore for this cause were the Nephites

contending with the Lamanites, to defend themselves, and their families, and their lands, their country, and their rights, and their religion. (Alma 43:46-47, see also Principle 4)

This is a good example of The Book of Mormon's *Art of War* Principle 16, and Joseph Smith's quote concerning revelation that is "...adapted to the circumstances in which the children of the kingdom are placed." (Teachings of the Prophet Joseph Smith, p. 256)

The important guideline in *this* principle is to respect those who have made a covenant of peace. In the Book of Mormon those who made a covenant of peace, and those warring Nephites who *did not* (such as Moroni, Helaman and their armies) worked together as brothers in the cause of Freedom. The Nephites protected the Ammonites (Anti-Nephi-Lehites) from death, while the Ammonites provided supplies and provisions to the Nephite armies (see Alma 27:23-24, and Alma 43:12-13). The sons of the Ammonites, who had NOT taken upon them the covenant of peace, became Helaman's 2,060 valiant stripling warriors, largely because of the righteousness of their parents (Alma 56:47-48). Would these warriors have been so disciplined and righteous had their parents NOT made a covenant of peace? There's always a connection in what the Lord inspires.

Other scriptures reaffirming this principle include Alma 24:19, Alma 43:12, Helaman 15:9-10.

Principle 21:

Let Your Enemy do your Work, when Possible

Sun Tzu says, "One cartload of the enemy's provisions is equivalent to twenty of one's own, and likewise a single PICUL (133 pounds) of his provender is equivalent to twenty from one's own store." (Sun Tzu II:15)

Whenever possible it is good practice to let an enemy's industry benefit your cause. Sun Tzu's multiplier of 20 shows this benefit to be quite staggering. It's recorded that the Nephites had the Lamanite prisoners of war bury the dead, dig ditches, build breastworks of timber, raise city defense systems, and build their own prisons. (see Alma 53:3-5) It would make sense, using Sun Tzu's ratio, that having their enemy do these things was equivalent to 20-fold of the Nephite army thus engaged.

Other scriptures reaffirming this principle include Alma 55:25, Alma 62:15.

Ending War: Transitioning into Peace

Principle 22:

Preach the Word of God to Prisoners of War

It's stunning, to this author, to see people everywhere attempt to find solutions to the ills of nations outside of God's word. All over the United States committees are meeting to curb suicide rates, help the mentally ill, and improve rehabilitation methods for law-breakers. We "ants" down here on planet Earth far too often look primarily to the wisdom and ideas of other ants. It seems to be that as soon as our thoughts and ideas for solutions rise to the level of heaven, we are reminded that our thinking is outside the box of acceptability, and that, from professional do-gooders—correct solutions are *only* to be found among the ants.

This author would remind the ants of the true doctrine that each of us are spiritually dead, which is defined as "separation from God's presence"; and what remedies come, or will ever come, from dead minds? There *is* hope of a spiritual resurrection, but how can this happen while we on Earth remain resistant to solutions that rise to the level of an all-knowing, all-wise, all-powerful, resurrected and glorified God?

> O that cunning plan of the evil one! O the vainness, and the frailties, and the foolishness of men! When they are learned they think they are wise, and they hearken not unto the counsel of God, for they set it aside, supposing they know of themselves, wherefore, their wisdom is foolishness and it profiteth them not. And they shall perish. But to be learned is good if they hearken unto the counsels of God. (2 Nephi 9:28-29)

The Book of Mormon's ancient missionaries knew this, and that:

> ...the preaching of the word had a great tendency to lead the people to do that which was just—yea, it had had more

> powerful effect upon the minds of the people than the sword, or anything else, which had happened unto them—therefore... it was expedient that they should try the virtue of the word of God. (Alma 31:5)

When an unrighteous leader, such as Amalickiah, stirs up the hearts of the people to anger against a perceived, yet innocent, "enemy", these stirred up subordinates, which represent the army's masses, will revert back to a position of peace if given the opportunity. All they need is to be convinced of the injustice of their cause. Time as a prisoner of war IS this opportunity. After Gidgiddoni and Lachoneus had imprisoned many of the Gadianton robbers, the record states that:

> ...when they had taken all the robbers prisoners, insomuch that none did escape who were not slain, they did cast their prisoners into prison, and did cause the word of God to be preached unto them; and as many as would repent of their sins and enter into a covenant that they would murder no more were set at liberty. But as many as there were who did not enter into a covenant, and who did still continue to

have those secret murders in their hearts, yea, as many as were found breathing out threatenings against their brethren were condemned and punished according to the law. (3 Nephi 5:4-5)

And they granted unto those robbers who had entered into a covenant to keep the peace of the land, who were desirous to remain Lamanites, lands, according to their numbers, that they might have, with their labors, wherewith to subsist upon; and thus they did establish peace in all the land. (3 Nephi 6:3)

This leads us to Principle 23.

Principle 23:

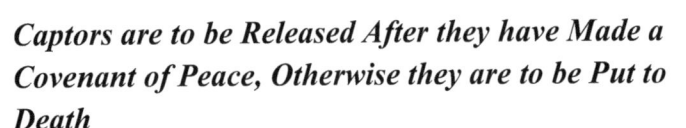

Captors are to be Released After they have Made a Covenant of Peace, Otherwise they are to be Put to Death

It is probably one of the most amazing doctrines of the Book of Mormon, yet even supported by Sun Tzu, that captured enemies are to be released pending an oath of peace—an oath that, in the Book of Mormon, wasn't "officially" recorded and didn't involve a team of lawyers scrutinizing stacks of legal documents.

From the very beginning of the Book of Mormon record, the taking of oaths was the most binding of contracts. Once Zoram had taken an oath to Nephi, he says "...our fears did cease concerning him." (1 Nephi 4:37)

As Moroni and Pahoran and their armies marched towards the city of Nephihah, with the intent to overthrow that city, they came across a "large body of men of the Lamanites." A scuffle ensued in which many Lamanites were slain, and the four-thousand that remained were taken prisoners of war. After this, the record states:

> ...after they had taken them, they caused them to enter into a covenant that they would no more take up their weapons of war against the Nephites. And when they had entered into this covenant they sent them to dwell with the people of Ammon, and they were in number about four thousand who had not been slain. (Alma 62:16-17)

Then the Nephites continued their march towards Nephihah, in which they, in the dead of night, let themselves down over the walls of the city, "thus when the morning came they were all within the walls of the city." (Alma 62:23)

Panic again ensued, and some of the Lamanites escaped, but the majority were taken prisoners of war. Yet again, the record states:

> "...that many of the Lamanites that were prisoners were desirous to join the people of Ammon and become a free people. And it came to pass that as many as were desirous, unto them it was granted according to their desires. Therefore, all the prisoners of the Lamanites did join the people of Ammon, and did begin to labor exceedingly, tilling the ground, raising all manner of grain, and flocks and herds of every kind..." (Alma 62:27-29)

From the record, Captain Moroni had a clear method of how to deal with an enemy, once captured. If his enemy would NOT give up his weapon of war, he was either compelled to do so and captured as a prisoner of war (Alma 52: 32, 36-39), or killed (see Alma 52:25, 44:14-20). If delivering up one's weapon of war was accompanied by a covenant of peace, he was released either to his own land (Alma 44:14-20), or, if he desired freedom, to the land of the Ammonites—a people and a land protected by the Nephite armies. (Alma 62:27-29)

Insurrections among their own countrymen were dealt with differently. (See Principles 6 & 16)

Sun Tzu tells us "Peace proposals **un**accompanied by a sworn covenant indicate a plot." (Sun Tzu IX:26)

Other scriptures reaffirming this principle include Alma 44:5-6, Alma 44:11- 20, Alma 50:35-36, Alma 52:25, 32, 37-39, Alma 57:14-15, Helaman 1:32-33, 3 Nephi 5:4-6, 3 Nephi 6:3.

Principle 24:

After a War is a Time of Humility, Fasting and Prayer, Giving Thanksgiving to God for the Victory, and to Mourn Lost Kindred

Perhaps there are few, if any, moments more cherished to any of God's children on Earth than those precious days immediately following a long, arduous, painstaking, yet victorious war—a victory which draws its due attention to the greatness and glory of almighty God in freedom's preservation. At the same time, settling into a society of peace doesn't come without a sacred remembrance of the cost—in fathers, sons, friends, and lost blood-brothers. After Gidgiddoni's and Lachoneus' victory over a vast army of Gadianton robbers, it's recorded that:

> ...they did break forth, all as one, in singing, and praising their God for the great thing which he had done for them, in preserving them from falling into the hands of their enemies. Yea, they did cry: Hosanna to the Most High God. And they did cry: Blessed be the name of the Lord God Almighty, the Most High God. And their hearts were swollen with joy, unto the gushing out of many tears, because of the great goodness of God in delivering them out of the hands of their enemies; and they knew it was because of their repentance and their humility that they had been delivered from an everlasting destruction.
>
> And now behold, there was not a living soul among all the people of the Nephites who did doubt in the least the

> words of all the holy prophets who had spoken… (3 Nephi 4:31-33, 3 Nephi 5:1)

Helaman describes his emotions, after being preserved by the hand of the Lord:

> I was filled with exceeding joy because of the goodness of God in preserving us, that we might not all perish; yea, and I trust that the souls of them who have been slain have entered into the rest of their God. (Alma 57:36)

Indeed, righteous warriors who have died in the defence of their freedom, and the freedom of others, are "happy" as indicated in Alma 56:11:

> Nevertheless, we may console ourselves in this point, that they have died in the cause of their country and of their God, yea, and they are happy. (Alma 56:11)

Other scriptures reaffirming this principle include Mosiah 2:4, Mosiah 24:21-22, Alma 45:1, Alma 49:28.

The Kingdom of God, by Brigham Young

A Discourse by President Brigham Young, Delivered in the Tabernacle, Great Salt Lake City, July 8, 1855. (Journal of Discourses, p. 309-317)

I will make a few remarks upon the same subject that was presented this forenoon, although there were many leading items in those remarks that would require a considerable length of time for me to give my views upon them, and to explain fully what I understand in relation to them. My brethren, who rise here to speak to the people, are also aware that it is impossible to fully explain to the congregation all the points that may be alluded to in a discourse.

Hence I design to speak a few words concerning the Kingdom of God. Not that I would disagree in the least from the remarks made by brothers Grant and Pratt, or that we differ in our views upon this subject. It is an extensive one, and the usual time never permits a person, in one short discourse, to fully explain such subjects as were presented for our edification this morning. I noticed throughout the remarks of both of the brethren that they did not make sufficient distinction, nor make it plain to the minds of the people, that the Kingdom of God would be different, in a certain sense, from all other kingdoms and empires upon the earth: this was for the want of time. In public speaking a man's mind is often led from one idea to another, branching to the right and to the left upon matters and points that need explanation, and I presume this is more particularly the case upon the subject of the Kingdom than any other.

If you and I could live in the flesh until that Kingdom is fully established, and actually spread abroad to rule in a temporal point of view, we should find that it will sustain and uphold every individual in what they deem their individual rights, so far as they do not infringe upon the rights of their fellow creatures. For instance, if the Kingdom of God was now established upon the continent of North and South America, and actually held rule and dominion over what we call the United States, the Methodist would be protected just as much as the Latter-day Saints; the Friend Quakers, the Shaking Quakers, and the members of every religious denomination would be sustained in what they considered to be their rights, so far as their notions were not incompatible with the laws of the Kingdom.

The Calvinist would be equally preserved in his rights, whether he believed, wished to believe, or said he believed and did not believe, that God has foreordained whatsoever comes to pass, and has dictated from all eternity the acts of the children of men down to the end of time, embracing every sin and every transgression of the law that has ever been committed upon the earth, from the first creation of man upon it; the Kingdom of God will protect him in that belief, and extend to him the privilege and the liberty of believing that, as fully as we should have the liberty of believing the opposite.

Again, men would come and say, "We believe in the Christian religion, but we firmly believe that the God we wish to serve has no eyes, no ears, no mouth, no head, and no body, that he is not composed of elements, that he has no parts nor passions, that his center is everywhere, his circumference nowhere; we firmly believe in serving such a God." That people would be preserved in their rights just as much as the people who believe that God lives, exists, and has the power of seeing, hearing, knowing, and understanding, and that we are organized and fashioned after, or, in other words, made like unto Him.

This is what the Kingdom of God will do for the inhabitants of the earth. If a sect should arise and say,

"We do not believe in a God at all, and only in that which we can see, hear, taste, and handle, that which we can understand, or in gods our own hands have made, which we have carved out of wood or stone, or cast from metal, we believe in serving only such god; we have many gods, we have a god for every element that has come within the range of our understanding, one for the air, the water, the sun, the moon, the different planets, and the stars; we have a god of war and a god of peace, which we carve out of wood and stone, or make them of silver, gold, iron, or copper, and put them in our temples. These are the gods we worship, and do not believe in any other god or gods"—even they would be preserved in their individual rights and belief, as much so as the Latter-day Saints.

When the Kingdom of God is fully set up and established on the face of the earth, and takes the pre-eminence over all other nations and kingdoms, it will protect the people in the enjoyment of all their rights, no matter what they believe, what they profess, or what they worship. If they wish to worship a god of their own workmanship, instead of the true and living God, all right, if they will mind their own business and let other people alone.

As was observed by brother Pratt, that Kingdom is actually organized, and the inhabitants of the earth do not know it. If this people know anything about it, all right; it is organized preparatory to taking effect in the due time of the Lord, and in the manner that shall please Him. As observed by one of the speakers this morning, that Kingdom grows out of the Church of Jesus Christ of Latter-day Saints, but it is not the Church, for a man may be a legislator in that body which will issue laws to sustain the inhabitants of the earth in their individual rights, and still not belong to the Church of Jesus Christ at all.

And further, though a man may not even believe in any religion, it would be perfectly right, when necessary, to give him the privilege of holding a seat among that body which will make laws to govern all the nations of the earth and control those who make no profession of religion at all; for that body would be governed, controlled, and dictated to acknowledge others in those rights which they wish to enjoy themselves. Then the Latter-day Saints would be protected, if a Kingdom of this kind was on the earth, the same as all other people.

It was observed this morning that the government of the United States was the best or most wholesome one on the earth, and the best adapted to our condition. That is very true. And if the Constitution of the United States, and the laws of the United States, and of the several States, were honored by the officers, by those who sit in judgment and dispense the laws to the people, yes, had even the letter of the law been honored, to say nothing of the spirit of it, of the spirit of right, it would have hung Governors, Judges, Generals, Magistrates, &c., for they violated the laws of their own States.

Such has been the case with our enemies in every instance that this people have been persecuted. If a person belonging to the Church of Jesus Christ of Latter-day Saints was guilty of stealing while living in the States, or if any of that Church were found guilty of murder, or any other transgression of the civil law, they ought to have been tried by the law, and have received the punishment affixed to the crime. Did any of the Latter-day Saints object to that? No, not one. Joseph the Prophet never objected to it, but on the contrary he urged it, prayed for it, and wished the Church to be delivered from all transgressors.

While we were in Illinois, if every transgressor of the law of that State, in our community, had been taken up and tried and punished, every Saint would have said, "Amen, we are better without than with them." So we say here, we are far better off without wicked men than with them. I would rather be in the midst of these mountains with one thousand, or even five hundred, men who are Latter-day Saints, than with five hundred thousand wicked men, in case all the forces of the earth were to come against us to battle, for God would fight the battles of the Saints, but He has not agreed to fight the battles of wicked men.

I say again that the Constitution, and laws of the United States, and the laws of the different States, as a general thing, are just as good as we want, provided they were honored. But we find Judges who do not honor the laws, yes, officers of the law dishonor the law. Legislators and lawmakers are frequently the first violators of the laws they make. "When the wicked rule the people mourn," and when the corruption of a people bears down the scale in favor of wickedness, that people is nigh unto destruction.

We have the proof on hand, that instead of the laws being honored, they have been violated in every instance of persecution against this people; instead of the laws being made honorable, they have been trampled under the feet of lawyers, judges, sheriffs, governors, legislators, and nearly all the officers of the government; such persons are the most guilty of breaking the laws.

To diverge a little, in regard to those who have persecuted this people and driven them to the mountains, I intend to meet them on their own grounds. It was asked this morning how we could obtain redress for our wrongs; I will tell you how it could be done, we could take the same law they have taken, viz., mobocracy, and if any miserable scoundrels come here, cut their throats. (All the people said, Amen.)

This would be meting out that treatment to wicked men, which they had measured to innocent persons. We could meet them on their own ground, when they will not honor the law, but will kill the Prophets and destroy the innocent. They could drive the innocent from their homes, take their houses and farms, cattle and goods, and destroy men, women, and children, walking over the laws of the United States, trampling them under their feet, and not honoring a single law.

Suppose I should follow the example they have shown us, and say, "Latter-day Saints, do ye likewise, and bid defiance to the whole clan of such men!" Some who are timid might say, "O! Our property will be destroyed, and we shall be killed." If any man here is a coward, there are fine mountain retreats for those who feel their hearts beating, at every little hue and cry of the wicked, as though they would break their ribs.

After this year we shall very likely again have fruitful seasons. Now, you cowards, if there are any, hunt in these mountains until you find some cavern where no person can find you, and go there and store up grain enough to last you and your families seven years; then when the mob comes, take your wives and your children, and creep into your den, and there remain until the war is over.

Do not apostatize to save your lives, for if you do, you are sure to lose them. You may do some good by laying up a little more grain than you want, and by handing out a biscuit to a brave hearted soldier passing by, hungry and fatigued. I could hide myself in these mountains, and defy five hundred thousand men to find me. That is not all, I could hide this whole people, and fifty times more, in the midst of these mountains, and our enemies might hunt until they died with old age, and they could not find us. You who are cowards, lay up your crops another year and hide them away.

You know that almost every time that Gentiles address us in public, they are very mindful to caution the Latter-day Saints "not to fight, now don't fight." Have we ever wanted to fight them? No, but we have wanted to preach to them the Gospel of peace.

Again, they say, "We are afraid that you, Latter-day Saints, are becoming aliens to the United States; we are afraid your hearts are weaned from the brotherhood down yonder." Don't talk about weaning now, for we were weaned long ago, that is, we are or should be weaned from all wickedness and wicked men. I am so perfectly weaned that when I embraced "Mormonism," I could have left father, mother, wife, children, and every relation I had, and am weaned from everybody that will turn a deaf ear to the voice of revelation. We are already weaned, but remember, we are not weaned from the Constitution of the United States, but only from wickedness, or at least we should be. Let every man and woman rise up in the strength of their God, and in their hearts ask no favors of the wicked; that is the way to live, and then let the wicked persecute, if they choose.

Are we going to fight? No, unless they come upon us and compel us either to fight or be slain.

Last fall we were visited by some of the brotherhood from the east, and I said, "Come in, my brother, come into my house; this is Mrs. Young, this is my daughter, and this is sister so and so. Wilford, Joseph, and William, open your houses and let these eastern brethren stay with us in comfortable quarters this winter." Wilford turns his family out of a fine house into a log cabin, to let the brotherhood in. Not a person, with but one exception, opened his house for their accommodation, without first asking my counsel. I said, "Yes, open your houses, turn out your wives and children, and let the brotherhood come in, and prove to the old stock, that we are their friends if they will do anything like what is decent;" and we furnished them comfortable winter quarters.

Directly the brotherhood began to pass around, and, as brother Grant said today, with a glove halfway on their fingers, apparently so virtuous in the daylight that they durst not touch a female's hand with theirs, unless gloved, but under the shadows of night they would go whisking around, here and there, saying, "Won't you take a sleigh ride with me this evening? Step into my carriage, and take a ride."

These proceedings were directly in the face and eyes of this people. What did they do when I introduced them to a wife, a daughter, or a sister, with all the grace, politeness, and kindness that could be expected from any man? As quick as my back was turned, it would be, "Miss, or Madam, I want to get into bed with you. Look here, you come to my office, won't you? I have a good bed there."

I will cut the matter short, and ask, once for all, did they return the compliment, and without exception reciprocate the kindness and courtesy with which they were invariably met? No, they did not, at least not all of them, for several returned evil for good, and introduced wickedness and corruption into our midst, and the Lord knows that we already had enough of that to contend with.

Past experience has taught the brethren that in future it will probably be the best policy to let soldiery quarter by themselves, and I am perfectly willing.

If persons come here and behave like gentlemen, they shall enjoy their rights, and we will enjoy ours or fight to the death. Let the laws of the United States be honored, and the laws of the individual States, and we will do as the Kingdom of God will do—protect everybody in their rights.

The experience of the last winter has taught us a good lesson, and we hope it has taught the people generally a lesson. I am troubled all the time with, "Brother Brigham," and "President Young, I do love you, President Young," when at the same time some, who use such expressions, will have one arm round my neck, loving me dearly, and the other around the neck of a scoundrel, trying to get Christ and Belial together; this I cannot endure.

If a man will keep a grog shop and permit wickedness to fester around him, or do anything else that is contrary to the Christian religion taught in the New Testament, I say to all such, either stop it, or take your property and leave, for our laws do not tolerate it, and we will put them in force against you. As to again suffering the wickedness and misrule of foul spirits that come into our midst, and are treated by us as gentlemen, I will not.

I will say to such official gentlemen as tell and boast "what the General Government is going to do," or "what they themselves will do," or "what they want to do," thinking to terrify the Latter-day Saints, that you may as well undertake to terrify the Almighty on His throne, as to terrify a Latter-day Saint of the true stripe—one who has the true blood in him.

True, there are many timid persons: timidity or fear is a weakness of the flesh; but to that person who has so far obtained the victory over the flesh as to know how God is dealing with the people, there is no terror, for he is just as ready to die as to live, just as the Lord pleases; his object is to do right, and he fears not.

The kingdom of heaven is at hand. Jesus taught his disciples to pray that the kingdom of heaven might come upon the earth, and when it does come, you will find that it will be very different from what many people are imagining or expecting it will be. Its spirit will be to preserve their individual rights sacred to the inhabitants of the earth.

What is the foundation of the rights of man? The Lord Almighty has organized man for the express purpose of becoming an independent being like unto Himself, and has given him his individual agency. Man is made in the likeness of his Creator, the great archetype of the human species, who bestowed upon him the principles of eternity, planting immortality within him, and leaving him at liberty to act in the way that seemeth good unto him, to choose or refuse for himself; to be a Latter-day Saint or a Wesleyan Methodist, to belong to the Church of England, the oldest daughter of the Mother Church, to the old Mother herself, to her sister the Greek Church, or to be an infidel and belong to no church.

As I have just stated, the Lord Almighty has organized every human creature for the express purpose of becoming independent, and has designed that they should be capable of receiving the principles of eternity to a fulness; and when they have received them unto a fulness, they are made perfect, like unto the Son of Man, and become Gods, even the Sons of God.

I am so far from believing that any government upon this earth has constitutions and laws that are perfect, that I do not even believe that there is a single revelation, among the many God has given to the Church, that is perfect in its fulness. The revelations of God contain correct doctrine and principle, so far as they go; but it is impossible for the poor, weak, low, groveling, sinful inhabitants of the earth to receive a revelation from the Almighty in all its perfections. He has to speak to us in a manner to meet the extent of our capacities, as we have to do with these benighted Lamanites; it would be of no benefit to talk to them as I am now speaking to you. Before you can enter into conversation with them and give them your ideas, you are under the necessity of condescending to their low estate, so far as communication is concerned, in order to exalt them.

You have to use the words they use, and address them in a manner to meet their capacities, in order to give them the knowledge you have to bestow. If an angel should come into this congregation, or visit any individual of it, and use the language he uses in heaven, what would we be benefited? Not any, because we could not understand a word he said. When angels come to visit mortals, they have to condescend to and assume, more or less, the condition of mortals, they have to descend to our capacities in order to communicate with us. I make these remarks to show you that the kingdom of heaven is not yet complete upon the earth. Why? Because the people are not prepared to receive it in its completeness, for they are not complete or perfect themselves.

The laws that the Lord has given are not fully perfect, because the people could not receive them in their perfect fulness; but they can receive a little here and a little there, a little today and a little tomorrow, a little more next week, and a little more in advance of that next year, if they make a wise improvement upon every little they receive; if they do not, they are left in the shade, and the light which the Lord reveals will appear darkness to them, and the kingdom of heaven will travel on and leave them groping. Hence, if we wish to act upon the fulness of the knowledge that the Lord designs to reveal, little by little, to the inhabitants of the earth, we must improve upon every little as it is revealed.

When He tells you how to purify your hearts, purify them. He says to the nations, "I send unto you my servants, I raise up unto you a Prophet, and call upon you, O inhabitants of the earth, through him, to repent of your sins." Do the people believe it is right to repent of their sins? Yes. How shall they repent of them? By forsaking them. If they will do this, the Lord will teach them how to become Saints. In what manner? By calling upon them through His servants to be baptized for the remission of sins, if they want to have their sins remitted, if they wish to be washed and made clean.

But before they go into the waters of baptism, they must forsake all their wicked practices, and covenant before the Lord to leave them forever behind them, saying, "Now we will go and serve the Lord our Maker." Has the Lord called upon the inhabitants of the earth in this way? Has He not taught you and me to become Latter-day Saints in this way? He has. Are we Saints still? When we first received the spirit of the Gospel, what was the world to us, with its grandeur, its riches, its elegance, its finery, its gaudy show, its glittering array of paltry honors, its empty titles, and everything pertaining to it? Nothing but a shadow, when the Lord opened our minds and by the visions of His Spirit revealed to us a few of the things He had in reserve for the faithful, which were only, as it were, a drop in the bucket, compared to the ocean yet to be revealed. Yet that little made our hearts leap for joy, and we felt that we could forsake everything for the knowledge of Jesus Christ and the perfections that we saw in his character.

Are you Saints still? If you are not, repent of your sins and do your first works. Has the Lord taught you how to consecrate yourselves to His service, build up His kingdom, and send forth the Gospel to the uttermost parts of the earth, that others may rejoice in the same Spirit that you have received, and enjoy the same things you enjoy? Yes, He has; and what more? A great deal more. He has taught you how to purify yourselves, and become holy, and be prepared to enter into His kingdom, how you can advance from one degree to another, and grow in grace and in the knowledge of the truth, until you are prepared to enter the celestial kingdom; how to pass every sentinel, watchman, and gatekeeper.

Then go on and build the Temples of the Lord, that you may receive the endowments in store for you, and possess the keys of the eternal Priesthood, that you may receive every word, sign, and token, and be made acquainted with the laws of angels, and of the kingdom of our Father and our God, and know how to pass from one degree to another, and enter fully into the joy of your Lord. Latter-day Saints, do you live to this, do you seek after it with all your heart? You are aware that the Lord is able to reveal all this in one day, but you could not understand it. The Elders who have preached abroad, and the Sisters who have taught their neighbors at home, know by experience that this is true.

When your minds have been lighted up with the candle of the Lord, and you have been able to speak forth the great things of God, things that were beyond the capacities of the people to receive, you have felt your ideas apparently rebound or return to you again. So it is with the Lord; He would be glad to send angels to communicate further to this people, but there is no room to receive it, consequently, He cannot come and dwell with you. There is a further reason—we are not capacitated to throw off in one day all our traditions, and our prepossessed feelings and notions, but have to do it little by little. It is a gradual process, advancing from one step to another; and as we lay off our false traditions and foolish notions, we receive more and more light, and thus we grow in grace; and if we continue so to grow we shall be prepared eventually to receive the Son of Man, and that is what we are after.

I wish to proceed a little further with regard to the Kingdom of God. The principles, doctrine, germ, and, I may say, marrow of that Kingdom are actually planted on the earth, but does it grow to perfection at once? No. When wheat is planted and germinates, you first see the blade, and by and by the head forming in the boot, from which in due time it bursts forth and makes its appearance. When this Kingdom is set up on the earth, and spreads, its condition is happily set forth in the toast that was given here on the fourth [of July], viz.—"May the wings of the American Eagle spread over the nations, and its down fall on America." Suppose the Kingdom of God is compared to the American Eagle; when it spreads over the nations, what will it do? Will it destroy every other bird that now flies, or that will fly? No, but they will exist the same as they do now. When the Kingdom of Heaven spreads over the whole earth, do you expect that all the people composing the different nations will become Latter-day Saints? If you do, you will be much mistaken.

Do you expect that every person will be destroyed from the face of the earth, but the Latter-day Saints? If you do, you will be mistaken. Many of our Elders labor under these erroneous expectations when reading over the sayings of the Apostles and Prophets in regard to the coming of the Son of Man. In one verse the Prophet will be describing the second Coming previous to the commencement of the Millennium, and perhaps in the same verse he will describe a scene that will take place after the Millennium, and when the earth will be cleansed from all wickedness, after Satan has been let loose a little season, and had another tour upon it, and after it is renovated and becomes sanctified, and is like a sea of glass, as John describes it. Will this be in the Millennium? No. But the order of society will be as it is when Christ comes to reign a thousand years; there will be every sort of sect and party, and every individual following what he supposes to be the best in religion, and in everything else, similar to what it is now.

Will there be wickedness then as now? No. How will you make this appear? When Jesus comes to rule and reign King of Nations as he now does King of Saints, the veil of the covering will be taken from all nations, that all flesh may see his glory together, but that will not make them all Saints. Seeing the Lord does not make a man a Saint, seeing an Angel does not make a man a Saint by any means. A man may see the finger of the Lord, and not thereby become a Saint; the veil of the covering may be taken from before the nations, and all flesh see His glory together, and at the same time declare they will not serve Him. They may, perhaps, feel something as a woman in Missouri did, who had been driven four times, and when she was about to be driven again she said, "I will be damned if I will stand it any longer; if God wants me to go through such a routine of things, He may take me where He pleases, and do with me as He pleases; I won't stand it any longer."

When the nations shall see the glory of God together, the spirit of their feelings may be couched in these words, "I will be damned if I will serve You." In those days, the Methodists and Presbyterians, headed by their priests, will not be allowed to form into a mob to drive, kill, and rob the Latter-day Saints; neither will the Latter-day Saints be allowed to rise up and say, "We will kill you Methodists, Presbyterians, etc.," neither will any of the different sects of Christendom be allowed to persecute each other.

What will they do? They will hear of the wisdom of Zion, and the kings and potentates of the nations will come up to Zion to inquire after the ways of the Lord, and to seek out the great knowledge, wisdom, and understanding manifested through the Saints of the Most High. They will inform the people of God that they belong to such and such a Church, and do not wish to change their religion.

They will be drawn to Zion by the great wisdom displayed there, and will attribute it to the cunning and craftiness of men. It will be asked, "What do you want to do, ye strangers from afar." "We want to live our own religion." "Will you bow the knee before God with us?" "O yes, we would as soon do it as not;" and at that time every knee shall bow, and every tongue acknowledge that God who is the framer and maker of all things, the governor and controller of the universe. They will have to bow the knee and confess that He is God, and that Jesus Christ, who suffered for the sins of the world, is actually its Redeemer; that by the shedding of his blood he has redeemed men, women, children, beasts, birds, fish, the earth itself, and everything that John saw and heard praising in heaven.

They will ask, "If I bow the knee and confess that he is that Savior, the Christ, to the glory of the Father, will you let me go home and be a Presbyterian?" "Yes."

"And not persecute me?" "Never." "Won't you let me go home and belong to the Greek Church?" "Yes." "Will you allow me to be a Friend Quaker, or a Shaking Quaker?" "O yes, anything you wish to be, but remember that you must not persecute your neighbors, but must mind your own business, and let your neighbors alone, and let them worship the sun, moon, a white dog, or anything else they please, being mindful that every knee has got to bow and every tongue confess. When you have paid this tribute to the Most High, who created you and preserves you, you may then go and worship what you please, or do what you please, if you do not infringe upon your neighbors."

The brethren who spoke this morning had not time to explain these points, and I have only just touched upon the subject.

The Church of Jesus Christ will produce this government, and cause it to grow and spread, and it will be a shield round about the Church. And under the influence and power of the Kingdom of God, the Church of God will rest secure and dwell in safety, without taking the trouble of governing and controlling the whole earth. The Kingdom of God will do this, it will control the kingdoms of the world.

When the day comes in which the Kingdom of God will bear rule, the flag of the United States will proudly flutter unsullied on the flag staff of liberty and equal rights, without a spot to sully its fair surface; the glorious flag our fathers have bequeathed to us will then be unfurled to the breeze by those who have power to hoist it aloft and defend its sanctity.

Up to this time we have carried the world on our backs. Joseph did it in his day, besides carrying this whole people, and now all this is upon my back, with my family to provide for at the same time, and we will carry it all, and bear off the Kingdom of God. And you may pile on state after state, and kingdom after kingdom, and all hell on top, and we will roll on the Kingdom of our God, gather out the seed of Abraham, build the cities and temples of Zion, and establish the Kingdom of God to bear rule over all the earth, and let the oppressed of all nations go free.

I have never yet talked as rough in these mountains as I did in the United States when they killed Joseph. I there said boldly and aloud, "If ever a man should lay his hands on me and say, on account of my religion, 'Thou art my prisoner,' the Lord Almighty helping me, I would send that man to hell across lots." I feel so now. Let mobbers keep their hands off from me, or I will send them where they belong; I am always prepared for such an emergency.

I have occupied time enough; may God bless you. Amen.

United States Foreign Policy, By Ezra Taft Benson

(Address delivered on June 21, 1968, at the Farm Bureau Banquet in Preston, Idaho)

> Observe good faith and justice towards all Nations; cultivate peace and harmony with all. Religion and Morality enjoin this conduct; and can it be, that good policy does not equally enjoin it? It will be worthy of a free, enlightened, and, at no distant period, a great Nation, to give to mankind the magnanimous and too novel example of a people always guided by an exalted justice and benevolence... Can it be that Providence has not connected the permanent felicity of a Nation with its Virtue?" President George Washington, Farewell Address, September 17, 1796

In the "Virginia Bill of Rights," drafted by George Mason and adopted by the Virginia Convention on

June 12, 1776, there appears this statement in Article 15:

> No free government, or the blessings of liberty, can be preserved to any people, but by a firm adherence to justice, moderation, temperance, frugality and virtue, and by frequent recurrence to fundamental principles. (Documents of American History, [Henry S. Commager, Editor], 1: 104)
>
> "The paramount need today," recently wrote David Lawrence, "is for the United States to clear the air by emphasizing fundamental principles. Until there are acts that implement those principles—not just words—diplomacy will accomplish nothing and the world will remain continually on the brink of war." (U.S. News and World Report, January 27, 1964)

It has been truly said that:

> We cannot clean up the mess in Washington, balance the budget, reduce taxes, check creeping Socialism, tell what is muscle or fat in our

> sprawling rearmament programs, purge subversives from our State Department, unless we come to grips with our foreign policy, upon which all other policies depend. (Senator Robert A. Taft, quoted by Phyllis Schlafly, A Choice Not An Echo, p. 26)

Ever since World War I, when we sent American boys to Europe supposedly to "make the world safe for democracy," our leaders in Washington have been acting as though the American people elected them to office for the primary purpose of leading the entire planet toward international peace, prosperity and one-world government. At times, these men appear to be more concerned with something called world opinion or with their image as world leaders than they are with securing the best possible advantage for us, that they are not "nationalistic" in their views, that they are willing to sacrifice narrow American interests for the greater good of the world community. Patriotism and America-first have become vulgar concepts within the chambers of our State Department. It is no wonder that the strength and prestige of the United States has slipped so low everywhere in the world.

In this connection, it is well to remember that on June 25, 1787, during the formulation of the Constitution at the Philadelphia Convention, Charles Pinckney, of South Carolina, made the famous speech in which he asserted:

> We mistake the object of our Government, if we hope or wish that it is to make us respectable abroad. Conquest or superiority among other powers is not or ought not ever to be the object of republican systems. If they are sufficiently active & energetic to rescue us from contempt & preserve our domestic happiness & security, it is all we can expect from them, – it is more than almost any other Government ensures to its citizens. (The Records of the Federal Convention [Max Farrand, Editor], 1: 402)

In his book, A Foreign Policy for Americans, the late Senator Robert A. Taft correctly reasoned that:

> No one can think intelligently on the many complicated problems of American foreign policy unless he decides first what he considers the real purpose and object of that policy... There has been no consistent purpose in our foreign policy for a good many

> years past. . . Fundamentally, I believe the ultimate purpose of our foreign policy must be to protect the liberty of the people of the United States. (p. 11)

There is one and only one legitimate goal of United States foreign policy. It is a narrow goal, a nationalistic goal: the preservation of our national independence. Nothing in the Constitution grants that the President shall have the privilege of offering himself as a world leader. He's our executive; he's on our payroll, in necessary; he's supposed to put our best interests in front of those of other nations. Nothing in the Constitution nor in logic grants to the President of the United States or to Congress the power to influence the political life of other countries, to "uplift" their cultures, to bolster their economies, to feed their peoples or even to defend them against their enemies. This point was made clear by the wise father of our country, George Washington:

> I have always given it as my decided opinion that no nation has a right to intermeddle in the internal concerns of another; that every one had a right to form and adopt whatever government they liked best to live under them selves; and that if this country could, consistent with its engagements,

> maintain a strict neutrality and thereby preserve peace, it was bound to do so by motives of policy, interest, and every other consideration. — George Washington (1732-1799) Letter to James Monroe (25 Aug. 1796)

The preservation of America's political, economic and military independence—the three cornerstones of sovereignty—is the sum and total prerogative of our government in dealing with the affairs of the world. Beyond that point, any humanitarian or charitable activities are the responsibility of individual citizens voluntarily without coercion of others to participate.

The proper function of government must be limited to a defensive role—the defense of individual citizens against bodily harm, theft and involuntary servitude at the hands of either domestic or foreign criminals. But to protect our people from bodily harm at the hands of foreign aggressors, we must maintain a military force which is not only capable of crushing an invasion, but of striking a sufficiently powerful counterblow as to make in unattractive for would-be conquerors to try their luck with us.

As President Washington explained in his Fifth Annual Address to both Houses of Congress:

> There is a rank due to the United States among nations, which will be withheld, if not absolutely lost, by the reputation of weakness. If we desire to avoid insult, we must be able to repel it; if we desire to secure the peace, one of the most powerful instruments of our rising prosperity, it must be known that we are at all times ready for war.
> (December 3, 1793; Writings 12:352)

He had earlier, in his First Annual Address, strongly warned that:

> To be prepared for war is one of the most effectual means of preserving peace. A free people ought not only to be armed, but disciplined. (January 8, 1790; Writings 11:456)

To protect our people from international theft, we must enter into agreements with other nations to abide by certain rules regarding trade, exchange of currency, enforcement of contracts, patent rights, etc. To protect our people against involuntary servitude or the loss of personal freedom on the international level, we must be willing to use our military might to help even one of our citizens no matter where he might be kidnapped or enslaved.

For those of you who have never heard or do not remember it, the story of Ion Perdicaris instructs us what an American President can and should do to protect the lives of its citizens. It seems that in the early years of the century, a North African bandit named Raisuli kidnapped Perdicaris, a naturalized American of Greek extraction.

> Teddy Roosevelt was our President at that time, and he knew just what to do. He did not "negotiate." And he did not send any "urgent requests." He simply ordered one of our gunboats to stand offshore, and sent the local sultan the following telegram: "Perdicaris alive, or Raisuli dead." They say Raisuli didn't waste any time getting a healthy Perdicaris down to the dock. (Review of the News, February 7, 1968, pp. 20-21)

Certainly we must avoid becoming entangled in a web of international treaties whose terms and clauses might reach inside our own borders and restrict our freedoms here at home. (2)

This is the defensive role of government expressed in international terms. Interestingly enough, these three aspects of national defense also translate directly into the three aspects of national sovereignty: military, economic and political.

Applying this philosophy to the sphere of foreign policy, one is able almost instantly to determine the correct answer to so many international questions that, otherwise, seem hopelessly complex. If the preservation and strengthening of our military, economic and political independence is the only legitimate objective of foreign policy decisions, then, at last, those decisions can be directed by a brilliant beacon of light that unerringly guides our ship of state past the treacherous reefs of international intrigue and into a calm open sea.

Should we disarm? And does it really make any difference whether we disarm unilaterally or collaterally? Either course of action would surrender our military independence. Should we pool our economic resources or our monetary system with those of other nations to create some kind of regional common market? It would constitute the surrender of our economic independence. Should we enter into treaties such as the U.N. Covenants which would obligate our citizens to conform their social behavior, their educational practices to rules and regulations set down by international agencies? Such treaty obligations amount to the voluntary and piece-meal surrender of our political independence. The answer to all such questions is a resounding "no," for the simple reason that the only way America can survive in this basically hostile and topsy-turvy world is to remain militarily, economically and politically strong and independent.

We must put off our rose-colored glasses, quit repeating those soothing but entirely false statements about world unity and brotherhood, and look to the world as it is, not as we would like it to become. Such an objective, and perhaps painful, survey leads to but one conclusion. We would be committing national suicide to surrender any of our independence, and chain ourselves to other nations in such a sick and turbulent world. President George Washington, in his immortal Farewell Address, explained our true policy in this regard:

> The great rule of conduct for us, in regard to foreign nations, is in extending our commercial relations to have with them as little political connection as possible... 'Tis our true policy to steer clear of permanent alliances, with any portion of the foreign world... Taking care always to keep ourselves, by suitable establishments on a respectably defensive posture, we may safely trust

> to temporary alliances for
> extraordinary emergencies.
> (September 17, 1796; Writings 13: 316-318; P.P.N.S., p. 547)

President Thomas Jefferson, in his First Inaugural Address, while discussing what he deemed to be "the essential principles of our government," (3) explained that as far as our relations with foreign nations are concerned this means:

> Equal and exact justice to all men, of whatever state or persuasion, religious or political; peace, commerce, and honest friendship with all nations—entangling alliances with none. . .
> (March 4, 1801; Works 8:4)

The world is smaller, you say? True, it is, but if one finds himself locked in a house with maniacs, thieves and murderers—even a small house—he does not increase his chances of survival by entering into alliances with his potential attackers and becoming dependent upon them for protection to the point where he is unable to defend himself. Perhaps the analogy between nations and maniacs is a little strong for some to accept. But if we put aside our squeamishness over strong language, and look hard at the real world in which we live, the analogy is quite sound in all but the rarest exceptions.

Already, I can hear the chorus chanting "Isolationism, isolationism, he's turning back the clock to isolationism." How many use that word without having the slightest idea of what it really means! The so-called isolationism of the United States in past decades is a pure myth. What isolationism? Long before the current trend of revoking our Declaration of Independence under the guise of international cooperation, American influence and trade was felt in every region of the globe. Individuals and private groups spread knowledge, business, prosperity, religion, good will and, above all, respect throughout every foreign continent. It was not necessary then for America to give up her independence to have contact and influence with other countries. It is not necessary now. Yet, many Americans have been led to believe that our country is so strong that it can defend, feed and subsidize half the world, while at the same time believing that we are so weak and "inter-dependent" that we cannot survive without pooling our resources and sovereignty with those we subsidize. If wanting no part of this kind of "logic" is isolationism, then it is time we brought it back into vogue.

Senator Robert A. Taft clearly explained our traditional foreign policy:

> Our traditional policy of neutrality and non-interference with other nations was based on the principle that this policy was the best way to avoid disputes with other nations and to maintain the liberty of this country without war. From the days of George Washington that has been the policy of the United States. It has never been isolationism; but it has always avoided alliances and interference in foreign quarrels as a preventive against possible war, and it has always opposed any commitment by the United States, in advance, to take any military action outside of our territory. It would leave us free to interfere or not according to whether we consider the case of sufficiently vital interest to the liberty of this country. It was the policy of the free hand. (A Foreign Policy for Americans, p. 12)

"But that is nationalism," chants the chorus. "And nationalism fosters jealousy, suspicion and hatred of other countries which in turn leads to war." (4) How many times has this utter nonsense been repeated without challenge as though it were some kind of empirical and self-evident truth! What kind of logic assumes that loving one's country means jealousy, suspicion and hatred of all others? Why can't we be proud of America as an independent nation and also have a feeling of brotherhood and respect for other peoples around the world? As a matter of fact, haven't Americans done just that for the past 200 years? What people have poured out more treasure to other lands, opened their doors to more immigrants, and sent more missionaries, teachers and doctors than we? Are we now to believe that love of our own country will suddenly cause us to hate the peoples of other lands?

It was the late Herbert Hoover who pointed out the social poison in the current derision of American nationalism:

> We must realize the vitality of the great spiritual force which we call nationalism. The fuzzy-minded intellectuals have sought to brand nationalism as a sin against mankind. They seem to think that infamy is attached to the word "nationalist." But that force cannot be obscured by denunciation of it as greed or selfishness—as it sometimes is. The spirit of nationalism springs from the

deepest of human emotions. It rises from the yearning of men to be free of foreign domination, to govern themselves. It springs from a thousand rills of race, of history, of sacrifice and pride in national achievement. (Quoted by Eugene W. Castle, Billions, Blunders and Baloney, p. 259)

In order for a man to be a good neighbor within his own community, he had better first love his own family before he tries to save the neighborhood. If he doesn't love his own, why should we believe he would love others?

Many well-intentioned people are now convinced that we are living in a period of history which makes it both possible and necessary to abandon our national sovereignty, to merge our nation militarily, economically, and politically with other nations, and to form, at last a world government which, supposedly, would put an end to war. We are told that this is merely doing between nations what we did so successfully with our thirteen colonies. This plea for world federalism is based on the idea that the mere act of joining separate political units together into a larger federal entity will somehow prevent those units from waging war with each other. The success of our own federal system is most often cited as proof that this theory is valid. But such an evaluation is a shallow one.

First of all, the American Civil War, one of the most bloody in all history, illustrates that the mere federation of governments, even those culturally similar, as in America, does not automatically prevent war between them. Secondly, we find that true peace quite easily exists between nations which are not federated. As a matter of fact, members of the British Commonwealth of Nations seemed to get along far more peacefully after the political bonds between them had been relaxed. In other words, true peace has absolutely nothing to do with whether separate political units are joined together—except, perhaps, that such a union may create a common military defense sufficiently impressive to deter an aggressive attack. But that is peace between the union and outside powers; it has little effect on peace between the units, themselves, which is the substance of the argument for world government.

Peace is the natural result of relationships between groups and cultures which are mutually satisfactory to both sides. These relationships are found with equal ease within or across federal lines. As a matter of fact, they are the relationships that promote peaceful conditions within the community and think for a moment; if you were marooned on an island with two other people, what relationships between you would be mutually satisfactory enough to prevent you from resorting to violence in your relationship? Or, to put it the other way around, what would cause you to break the peace and raise your hand against your partners?

Obviously, if one or both of the partners attempted to seize your food and shelter, you would fight. Their reaction to similar efforts on your part would be the same. If they attempted to take away your freedom, to dictate how you would conduct your affairs, or tell you what moral and ethical standards you must follow, likewise, you would fight. And if they constantly ridiculed your attire, your manners and your speech, in time you might be sparked into a brawl. The best way to keep the peace on that island is for each one to mind his own business, to respect each other's right to be different (even to act in a way that seems foolish or improper, if he wishes), and to have compassion for each other's troubles and hardships—but not to force each other to do something! And, to make sure that the others hold to their end of the bargain, each should keep physically strong enough to make any violation of this code unprofitable. (5)

Now, suppose these three got together and decided to form a political union, to "federate" as it were. Would this really change anything? Suppose they declared themselves to be the United Persons, and wrote a charter, and held daily meetings and passed resolutions. What then? These superficial ceremonies might be fun for awhile, but the minute two of them out-voted the other, and started "legally" to take his food and shelter, limit his freedom or force him to accept an unwanted standard of moral conduct, they would be right back where they all began. Federation or no federation, they would fight.

Is it really different between nations? Not at all. The same simple code of conduct applies in all human relationships, large or small. Regardless of the size, be it international or three men on an island, the basic unit is still the human personality. Ignore this fact, and any plan is doomed to failure. (6)

It might be worthwhile at this point to mention that Washington's policy of neutrality and non-interference was adhered to by those who followed him. For instance, President John Adams, in his Inaugural Address, resolved "to do justice as far as may depend upon me, at all times and to all nations, and maintain peace, friendship, and benevolence with all the world." He later said, in a special message to Congress:

It is my sincere desire, and in this I presume I concur with you and with our constituents, to preserve peace and friendship with all nations...

To which the Senate, presided over by Thomas Jefferson, replied:

> Peace and harmony with all nations is our sincere wish; but such being the lot of humanity that nations will not always reciprocate peaceable dispositions, it is our firm belief that effectual measures of defense will tend to inspire that national self-respect and confidence at home which is the unfailing source of respectability abroad, to check aggression and prevent war. (Quoted by Clarence B. Carson, The American Tradition, p. 210)

When the thirteen colonies formed our Federal Union, they had two very important factors in their favor, neither of which are present in the world at large today. First, the colonists themselves were all of a similar cultural background. They enjoyed similar legal systems, they spoke the same language, and they shared similar religious beliefs. They had much in common. The second advantage, and the most important of the two, was that they formed their union under a constitution which was designed to prevent any of them, or a majority of them, from forcefully intervening in the affairs of the others. The original federal government was authorized to provide mutual defense, run a post office, and that was about all. As previously mentioned, however, even though we had these powerful forces working in our favor, full scale war did break out at one tragic point in our history.

The peace that followed, of course, was no peace at all, but was only the smoldering resentment and hatred that follows in the wake of any armed conflict. Fortunately, the common ties between North and South, the cultural similarities and the common heritage, have proved through the intervening years to over-balance the differences. And with the gradual passing away of the generation that carried the battle scars, the Union has healed.

Among the nations of the world today, there are precious few common bonds that could help overcome the clash of cross-purposes that inevitably must arise between groups with such divergent ethnic, linguistic, legal, religious, cultural, and political environments. To add fuel to the fire, the concept woven into all of the present-day proposals for world government (The U.N. foremost among these) is one of unlimited governmental power to impose by force a monolithic set of values and conduct on all groups and individuals whether they like it or not. Far from insuring peace, such conditions can only enhance the chances of war. (7)

In this connection it is interesting to point out that the late J. Reuben Clark, who was recently described as "probably the greatest authority on [the Constitution] during the past fifty years" (American Opinion, April 1966, p. 113), in 1945–the year the United Nations charter was adopted–made this prediction in his devastating and prophetic "cursory analysis" of the United Nations Charter:

There seems no reason to doubt that such real approval as the Charter has among the people is based upon the belief that if the Charter is put into effect, wars will end. . . The Charter will not certainly end war. Some will ask – why not? In the first place, there is no provision in the Charter itself that contemplates ending war. It is true the Charter provides for force to bring peace, but such use of force is itself war. . . It is true the Charter is built to prepare for war, not to promote peace. . . The Charter is a war document, not a peace document.

> Not only does the Charter Organization not prevent future wars, but it makes it practically certain that we will have

> future wars, and as to such wars it takes from us the power to declare them, to choose the side on which we shall fight, to determine what forces and military equipment we shall use in the war, and to control and command our sons who do the fighting.
> (Unpublished Manuscript; quoted in P.P.N.S., p. 458)

Everyone is for peace and against war—particularly the horrors of nuclear war. And what are the horrors of war? Why, death, destruction and human suffering, of course! But, wait a minute. Since the big "peace" began at the end of World War II, isn't it a fact that, behind the iron and bamboo curtains, there has been more death, destruction and human suffering than in most of the big wars of history combined? Yes, it is a fact—a horrible fact—which Martin Dies, the former long-time Chairman of the House Committee on Un-American Activities, described in these words:

In Russia, a minimum of 25,000,000 people have been starved to death and murdered in 45 years. In Red China, the figure is probably at least 35,000,000 in a short 12 years. These ruthless, inhuman atrocities have been investigated, documented and reported in print, by numerous committees of the Congress. Yet only a relative handful of Americans know where to look for the facts, or even know the reports exist; and still fewer have read them. (The Martin Dies Story, p. 20)

A consideration of these facts means that we have to redefine our terms when we talk about "peace." There are two kinds of peace. If we define peace as merely the absence of war, then we could be talking about the peace that reigns in a communist slave labor camp. The wretched souls in prison there are not at war, but do you think they would call it peace?

The only real peace—the one most of us think about when we use the term—is a peace with freedom. A Nation that is not willing, if necessary, to face the rigors of war to defend its real peace-in-freedom is doomed to lose both its freedom and its peace! These are the hard facts of life. We may not like them, but until we live in a far better world than exists today, we must face up to them squarely and courageously. (8)

In a discussion of war and its effects these wise words of James Madison should always be remembered:

> Of all the enemies to public liberty war is, perhaps, the most to be dreaded, because it comprises and develops the germ of every other. War is the parent of armies; from these proceed debts

and taxes; and armies, and debts, and taxes are the known instruments for bringing the many under the domination of the few. In war, too, the discretionary power of the Executive is extended; its influence in dealing out offices, honors, and emoluments is multiplied; and all the means of seducing the minds, are added to those of subduing the force, of the people. The same malignant aspect in republicanism may be traced in the inequality of fortunes, and the opportunities of fraud, growing out of a state of war, and in the degeneracy of manners and of morals, engendered by both. No nation could preserve its freedom in the midst of continual warfare.... (April 20, 1795; Works 4:491-2; P.P.N.S., p. 468)

Shortly after this, in a letter to Thomas Jefferson, James Madison issued another warning which should never be forgotten:

The management of foreign relations appears to be the most susceptible of abuse, of all the trusts committed to a Government, because they can be concealed or disclosed, or disclosed in such parts & at such times as will best suit particular views; and because the body of the people are less capable of judging & are more under the influence of prejudices, on that branch of their affairs, than of any other. Perhaps it is a universal truth that the loss of liberty at home is to be charged to provisions against danger real or pretended from abroad. (May 13, 1798; Works 2:140-1; P.P.N.S., p. 431)

Until all nations follow the concept of limited government, it is unlikely that universal peace will ever be realized on this planet. Unlimited, power-grasping governments will always resort to force if they think they can get away with it. (9) But there can be peace for America. As long as our leaders faithfully discharge their duty to preserve and strengthen the military, economic and political independence of our Republic, the world's petty despots will leave us alone. What more could we ask of U.S. foreign policy?

From these primary policy pronouncements some general principles emerge. They can be reduced to a few heads and stated as imperatives in the following manner:

The United States should:

- Establish and maintain a position of independence with regard to other countries
- Avoid political connection, involvement or intervention in the affairs of other countries
- Make no permanent or entangling alliances
- Treat all nations impartially, neither granting nor accepting special privileges from any
- Promote commerce with all free peoples and countries
- Cooperate with other countries to develop civilized rules of intercourse
- Act always in accordance with the "laws of Nations"
- Remedy all just claims of injury to other nations and require just treatment from other nations, standing ready, if necessary to punish offenders
- Maintain a defensive force of sufficient magnitude to deter aggressors. (10) (See The American Tradition, p. 212)

For the first hundred years and more of the existence of the Republic, Americans developed and maintained a tradition that was in keeping with the above principles. We can say with confidence that the United States established a tradition of foreign relations in keeping with the principles laid down by the founding fathers. In the words of Senator Taft:

> I do not believe it a selfish goal for us to insist that the over-riding purpose of all American foreign policy should be the maintenance of the liberty and the peace of the people of the United States, so that they may achieve that intellectual and material improvement which is their genius and in which they can do an even greater service to mankind than we can by billions of material assistance—and more than we can ever do by war. (A Foreign Policy For Americans, p. 14)

It seems fitting in conclusion to refer you again to the inspired words of the wise father of our country. He said:

> My ardent desire is, and my aim has been. . . to keep the United States free

from political connections with every other country, to see them independent of all and under the influence of none. In a word, I want an American character, that the powers of Europe may be convinced we act for ourselves, and not for others. This, in my judgment, is the only way to be respected abroad and happy at home. (October 9, 1795; Writings 13:119)

Endnotes

1. Address delivered on June 21, 1968, at the Farm Bureau Banquet in Preston, Idaho.

2. "Against the insidious wiles of foreign influence, I conjure you to believe me, my fellow-citizens, the jealousy of a free people ought to be constantly awake, since history and experience prove that foreign influence is one of the most baneful foes of republican Government. —But that jealousy, to be useful, must be impartial; else it becomes the instrument of the very influence to be avoided, instead of a defense against it." (President George Washington, Farewell Address, September 17, 1796; Writings 13:315)

3. "About to enter, fellow-citizens, on the exercise of duties which comprehend everything dear and valuable to you, it is proper you should understand what I deem the essential principles of our Government, and consequently those which ought to shape its Administration. I will compress them within the narrowest compass they will bear, stating the general principle, but not all its limitations. Equal and exact justice to all men, of whatever state or persuasion, religious or political; peace, commerce, and honest friendship with all nations, entangling alliances with none; the support of the State governments in all their rights, as the most competent administrations for our domestic concerns and the surest bulwarks against anti-republican tendencies; the preservation of the General Government in its whole constitutional vigor, as the sheet anchor of our peace at home and safety abroad; a jealous care of the right of election by the people—a mild and safe corrective of abuses which are lopped by the sword of revolution where peaceable remedies are not provided; absolute acquiescence in the decisions of the majority, the vital principle of republics, from which is no appeal but to force, the vital principle and immediate parent of despotism; a well disciplined militia, our best reliance in peace and for the first moments of war, till regulars may relieve them; the supremacy of the civil over the military authority;

economy in the public expense, that labor may be lightly burdened; the honest payment of our debts and sacred preservation of the public faith; encouragement of agriculture, and of commerce as its handmaid; the diffusion of information and arraignment of all abuses at the bar of the public reason; freedom of religion; freedom of the press, and freedom of person under the protection of the habeas corpus, and trial by juries impartially selected. These principles form the bright constellation which has gone before us and guided our steps through an age of revolution and reformation. The wisdom of our sages and blood of our heroes have been devoted to their attainment. They should be the creed of our political faith, the text of civic instruction, the touchstone by which to try the services of those we trust; and should we wander from them in moments of error or of alarm, let us hasten to retrace our steps and to regain the road which alone leads to peace, liberty, and safety. (Thomas Jefferson, First Inaugural Address, March 4, 1801; also known as the Creed of our Political Faith; Works 8:4-5)

4. Credit is given to G. Edward Griffin, The Fearful Master, for some of the thoughts expressed in this chapter.

5. "It takes a combination of three factors to protect our national interests under all conditions and to

maintain peace on our terms. The three factors are: credible military superiority along the entire spectrum of modern warfare; courageous and decisive diplomacy; and the active support of the American people." (General Thomas S. Power, Design for Survival, p. 6)

6. "Those who have written on civil government lay it down as a first principle, and all historians demonstrate the same, that whoever would found a state and make proper laws for the government of it must presume that all men are bad by nature: that they will not fail to show that natural depravity of heart whenever they have a fair opportunity. . . constant experience shows us that every man vested with power is apt to abuse it. He pushes on till he comes to something that limits him." (Machiavelli, 1469-1527; quoted by John Adams, Works 4:408)

7. "Power and law are not synonymous. In truth they are frequently in opposition and irreconcilable. There is God's Law from which all Equitable laws of man emerge and by which men must live if they are not to die in oppression, chaos and despair. Divorced from God's eternal and immutable Law, established before the founding of the suns, man's power is evil no matter the noble words with which it is employed or the motives urged when enforcing it. Men of good will, mindful therefore of the Law laid down by God,

will oppose governments whose rule is by men, and if they wish to survive as a nation they will destroy the government which attempts to adjudicate by the whim of venal judges." (Cicero, quoted in A Pillar of Iron, p. ix)

8. It is our duty. . . to endeavor to avoid war; but if it shall actually take place, no matter by whom brought on, we must defend ourselves. If our house be on fire, without inquiring whether it was fired from within or without, we must try to extinguish it." (Thomas Jefferson, to James Lewis, May 9, 1798; Works 4:241)

9. "There is one safeguard known generally to the wise, which is an advantage and security to all, but especially to democracies as against despots. What is it? Distrust." (Demosthenes, 384-322 B.C.; Familiar Quotations, p. 277)

10. "Deterrence is more than bombs and missiles and tanks and armies. Deterrence is a sound economy and prosperous industry. Deterrence is scientific progress and good schools. Deterrence is effective civil defense and the maintenance of law and order. Deterrence is the practice of religion and respect for the rights and convictions of others. Deterrence is a high standard of morals and wholesome family life. Deterrence is honesty in public office and freedom of the press. Deterrence is all these things and many

more, for only a nation that is healthy and strong in every respect has the power and will to deter the forces from within and without that threaten its survival." (General Thomas S. Power, Design for Survival, p. 242)

Constitutional State Militia
BILL *(Idaho example for all states)*

WHEREAS, Article IV, Section 4 of the U.S. Constitution states "The United States shall guarantee to every state in this Union a Republican form of government"; and

WHEREAS, The 2nd Amendment to the Constitution declares that "A well-regulated militia [is] necessary to the security of a free state,"; and

WHEREAS, Idaho's House Joint Memorial No. 4 (2009), declared a ***State Declaration of Independence from the Federal Government when the two governmental entities differ*** by saying "TO THE PRESIDENT OF THE UNITED STATES, THE SENATE AND HOUSE OF REPRESENTATIVES OF THE UNITED STATES IN CONGRESS ASSEMBLED, AND THE CONGRESSIONAL DELEGATION REPRESENTING THE STATE OF IDAHO IN THE CONGRESS OF THE UNITED STATES that:

1. **WHEREAS**, Section 2, Article I, of the Constitution of the State of Idaho, sets forth the Declaration of Rights and reads as follows: "All political power is inherent in the people. Government is instituted for their equal protection and benefit, and they have the right to alter, reform or abolish the same whenever

they may deem it necessary; and no special privileges or immunities shall ever be granted that may not be altered, revoked, or repealed by the legislature."; and

2. **WHEREAS**, the Tenth Amendment to the Constitution of the United States reads as follows: "The powers not delegated to the United States by the Constitution, nor prohibited by it to the States, are reserved to the States respectively, or to the people."; and

3. **WHEREAS**, the Tenth Amendment defines the total scope of federal power as being that specifically granted by the Constitution of the United States and no more; and

4. **WHEREAS**, the scope of power defined by the Tenth Amendment means that the federal government was created by the states specifically to be an agent of the states; and

5. **WHEREAS**, today, in 2009, the states are demonstrably treated as agents of the federal government; and

6. **WHEREAS**, many federal mandates are directly in violation of the Tenth Amendment to the Constitution of the United States; and

7. **WHEREAS**, the United States Supreme Court has ruled in New York v. United States, 505 U.S. 144 (1992), that Congress may not simply commandeer the legislative and regulatory processes of the states;and

8. **NOW, THEREFORE, BE IT RESOLVED** by the members of the First Regular Session of the Sixtieth Idaho Legislature, the House of

Representatives and the Senate concurring therein, that the state of Idaho hereby claims sovereignty under the Tenth Amendment to the Constitution of the United States over all powers not otherwise enumerated and granted to the federal government by the Constitution of the United States.

9. **BE IT FURTHER RESOLVED** that this serves as notice and demand to the federal government, as our agent, to cease and desist, effective immediately, mandates that are beyond the scope of these constitutionally delegated powers. (Article I, Sec. 8, Clauses 2 -17)
10. **BE IT FURTHER RESOLVED** that all compulsory federal legislation that directs states to comply under threat of civil or criminal penalties or sanctions, or requires states to pass legislation or lose federal funding, be prohibited.

and

WHEREAS, Our Nation's original Declaration of Independence was reinforced by George Washington and the Continental Army; and

WHEREAS, Justice Joseph Story stated in his Commentaries on the Constitution 3:§§ 1833 the truth that:

- "The militia is the natural defence of a free country against sudden foreign invasions, domestic insurrections, and domestic usurpations of power by rulers." And

- *"The right of the citizens to keep and bear arms has justly been considered, as the palladium of the liberties of a republic; since it offers a strong moral check against the usurpation and arbitrary power of rulers*; and will generally, even if these are successful in the first instance, enable the people to resist and triumph over them. Yet, though this truth would seem so clear, and the importance of a well regulated militia would seem so undeniable, it cannot be disguised, that among the American people there is a growing indifference to any system of militia discipline, and a strong disposition, from a sense of its burthens, to be rid of all regulations."

and

WHEREAS, Title 46-103 in the Idaho Statutes states: "The militia of the state of Idaho shall be divided into three (3) classes, to wit: The National Guard, the organized militia, and the unorganized militia." and

WHEREAS, Title 46-103 in the Idaho Statutes further states: "The organized militia shall include any portion of the unorganized militia called into service by the governor, and not federally recognized. The unorganized militia shall include all of the militia of the state of Idaho not included in the national guard or the organized militia."; and

WHEREAS, ARTICLE XIV Section 1 of the CONSTITUION OF THE STATE OF IDAHO states: "All able-bodied male persons, residents of this state, between the ages of eighteen and forty-five years, shall be enrolled in the militia"; and

WHEREAS, ARTICLE XIV Section 2 of the CONSTITUION OF THE STATE OF IDAHO states: "The legislature shall provide by law for the enrolment, equipment and discipline of the militia, to conform as nearly as practicable to the regulations for the government of the armies of the United States, and pass such laws to promote volunteer organizations as may afford them effectual encouragement."; and

WHEREAS, ARTICLE XIV Section 6 of the CONSTITUION OF THE STATE OF IDAHO states: "No armed police force, or detective agency, or armed body of men, shall ever be brought into this state for the suppression of domestic violence except upon the application of the legislature, or the executive, when the legislature cannot be convened."; and

WHEREAS, No such provisions currently exist as per ARTICLE XIV Section 1 and 2 of the CONSTITUION OF THE STATE OF IDAHO pertaining to:

- An enrollment of able-bodied male persons between the ages of eighteen and forty-five years
- Equipment and discipline of Organized and Unorganized militias
- Passing laws to promote and encourage volunteering for Organized and Unorganized militias

THEREFORE, be it resolved that Idaho's general officers, including Idaho's Governor, shall appoint such a person as fit and able to reactivate Idaho's Organized and Unorganized militias, and support this person, along with 5 staff members, in recruiting, training, equipping, and funding for Organized and Unorganized militias as described by Idaho law and pursuant to defending the people in Idaho for such threats which are reasonable, and which may come from enemies foreign and domestic, or which may come from "sudden foreign invasions, domestic insurrections, and domestic usurpations of power by rulers," as per Joseph Story's quote above.

AFTERWORD

By Farley Anderson

The Book of Mormon is as the prophet Joseph said, "The most correct book." It is doubtful this is in reference to the book's form. Rather, the power of the book is in its ability to correct that which is amiss. Kelly Gneiting has hit the nail on the head in his hypothesis, research, and logically delivered writ. This is a powerful reading and reference book!

I greatly enjoyed the review of Sun Tzu's Art of War at the very time my mind was centered on the gospel principles necessary to face the greatest possible test, extreme challenge, and ultimate learning experience, which is war. Knowing that the Book of Mormon was written for us and that so much of this text deals with war should tell us something of what is in store in battles yet to be fought.

The wisdom contained in this book is equally valuable to fight and win our daily spiritual and physical battles. The war in heaven continues in the here and now and is currently upon us. To be ignorant of the correct principles of warfare is to put us in great jeopardy.

Gneiting has put tools of thought at our disposal. When the prophesied time of the great battle is upon us, I would want to be well versed in the principles of this book. We will face the scenario of Isaiah chapter 59. The enemy will come upon us as a flood. The fear of the Lord will arise from the west. The Lord shall lift up a standard unto his people. And we shall experience the fulfillment of the covenant that the Redeemer shall come to Zion. Knowing how it shall turn out, let us prepare to play our part!

Thank you, Kelly Gneiting, for the gift of this book.

Farley Anderson,
Issues Committee
Independent American Party

A final Poem, 'The Faith of a Patriot'

Humble, meek, submissive, yet strong,
With a knowledge of truth of right and wrong;
He looks o'er the land—endless fields in view;
Seeing a harvest great, but laborers few.

His scene is the deep, amid black skies,
and a ten-horned beast, from the sea doth rise;
At this terrible view, some friends now cower,
and submit to the beast in this self-same hour.

But a mightier image comes into view,
And a voice for a cause which beckons the few;
The invisible image of a mighty hand,
And an outstretched arm, on behalf of man.

With sword now drawn, he makes his choice,

to lend to the cause, heart, soul, and voice;

And says to himself, while others flee,

"I can do all things through Christ, who strengthens me."

  While the beast approaches with its seven crowns,

thru the quaking earth and the shrill of sounds;

A battle is fought for humanity,

To keep our home brave—ensure our land free.

  Then despite works of Marx, and Gadianton bands,

The conspiracy is thwarted throughout all lands;

And all joyfully gaze, while freedom spreads,

At the lifeless beast, with its seven heads.

Internal Bleeding

For people that really want to live!

Noel McLean

authorHOUSE®

AuthorHouse™ UK Ltd.
500 Avebury Boulevard
Central Milton Keynes, MK9 2BE
www.authorhouse.co.uk
Phone: 08001974150

© 2010 Noel McLean. All rights reserved.

No part of this book may be reproduced, stored in a retrieval system, or transmitted by any means without the written permission of the author.

First published by AuthorHouse 3/16/2010

ISBN: 978-1-4490-6294-1 (sc)

Scripture taken from the New King James Version.
Copyright © 1982 by Thomas Nelson, Inc.
Used by permission. All rights reserved.

This book is printed on acid-free paper.

Dedication

*"As in water, face reflects face,
so a man's heart reveals the man"*
Proverbs 27:19

    This book is dedicated to those who tirelessly serve and sacrifice in order to help and support others around them. The daily heroes who parent, help the weak, teach and inspire people. The people who somehow against the odds and despite their personal wounds, continue to touch lives with their gift but have now reached a place where they know they now need someone to lovingly help them receive they very restoration and healing they helped others to receive. This book is a recognition of your greatness but also a recognition of your inner needs.

Contents

Acknowledgements 5
Introduction 7

SECTION 1   **DIAGNOSIS**

Chapter 1	Some of the Time	13
Chapter 2	Who Am I?	18
Chapter 3	Help I'm Bleeding!	25
Chapter 4	I Refuse To Cry!	33
Chapter 5	Fake It Until You Make It!	37
Chapter 6	The Talent Trap	46
Chapter 7	Is Your Blood Speaking?	53
Chapter 8	It Did Matter!	61

SECTION 2   **PREPARING FOR SURGERY**

Chapter 9	Don't Cut Yourself!	66
Chapter 10	Getting Past Your 'Never Agains'	70
Chapter 11	Jumping Out of the Wheel	76
Chapter 12	Quarantine	84

SECTION 3   **SURGERY**

Chapter 13	Time for Surgery	89
Chapter 14	My New World	96
Chapter 15	I'm Free!	109